MICH

DOUGLAS

MICHAEL
DOUGLAS

MICHAEL DOUGLAS

The unofficial and unauthorised biography of
MICHAEL DOUGLAS
by Adam Phillips

Published by
Kandour Ltd
1-3 Colebrook Place
London N1 8HZ

This edition printed in 2004 for
Bookmart Limited
Registered Number 2372865
Trading as Bookmart Ltd
Blaby Road
Wigston
Leicester LE18 4SE

First published June 2004

ISBN 1–904756–14–X

Production services:
Metro Media Ltd

Author: Adam Phillips

With thanks to: Jenny Ross, Emma Hayley,
Lee Coventry, Belinda Weber

Cover design: Mike Lomax
Cover Image: Rex Features

Inside Images: Rex Features

© Kandour Ltd

Printed and bound by Nørhaven Paperback, Denmark

MICHAEL DOUGLAS

FOREWORD

This series of biographies is a celebration of celebrity. It features some of the world's greatest modern-day icons including movie stars, soap personalities, pop idols, comedians and sporting heroes. Each biography examines their struggles, their family background, their rise to stardom and in some cases their struggle to stay there. The books aim to shed some light on what makes a star. Why do some people succeed when others fail?

Written in a light-hearted and lively way, and coupled with the most up-to-date details on the world's favourite heroes and heroines, this series is an entertaining read for anyone interested in the world of celebrity. Discover all about their career highlights – what was the defining moment to propel them into superstardom? No story about fame is without its ups and downs. We reveal the emotional rollercoaster ride that many of these stars have been on to stay at the top. Read all about your most adored personalities in these riveting books.

MICHAEL DOUGLAS

CONTENTS

MICHAEL DOUGLAS

FACT FILE

Full Name: Michael Kirk Douglas
Eye Colour: Blue
Date of Birth: 25 September 1944
Place Of Birth: New Jersey, USA
Height: 5' 9"
Marriages: Diandra Douglas (1977–1998)
Catherine Zeta-Jones (2000 – present day)
Children:
Son: Cameron, DJ and actor; mother,
Diandra Douglas, born 1978
Son: Dylan; mother, Catherine Zeta-Jones,
born 2000
Daughter: Carys; mother, Catherine Zeta-Jones,
born 2003

Star sign: Libra (23 September – 22 October)
Librans tend to be great achievers because of their
ability to think their way through problems. Their
generous spirit also means that they are happy to
share the spoils of war with those who have
helped them. Librans, though, are not happy in
confrontational scenes – in fact, only those who
learn how to deal with such situations will end up
achieving their maximum potential. Other famous
Librans include song-writer and singing legend
John Lennon and US daredevil Evil Knievel.

MICHAEL DOUGLAS

Chinese birth sign: Monkey

Blessed with natural intelligence, charisma and an appetite for challenge, they are known for their success and their towering self-belief. The downside is that they can be sly while feeling that they are above everyone else – and beyond reproach.

Career High:

In 1976 when he received the Best Picture Oscar for *One Flew Over The Cuckoo's Nest* and in 1988 for his performance as Gordon Gekko in *Wall Street* which garnered him an Oscar and Golden Globe for Best Actor. In 2004, he was awarded Cecil B. DeMille Award for outstanding contribution to the entertainment field at the 61st annual Golden Globe Awards.

MICHAEL DOUGLAS

DID YOU KNOW?

One of Michael Douglas's first jobs after leaving university was at a petrol station. Douglas threw himself into the job and has said that he drew genuine and immense satisfaction from being his "own man" as he drove tow-trucks and cleaned windscreens. And so much did he enjoy his job that he was awarded the heady honour of being made Mobil's Man Of The Month.

Catherine Zeta-Jones and Michael Douglas share the same birthday – 25 September.

1

A chip off the old block

MICHAEL DOUGLAS

A CHIP OFF THE OLD BLOCK

I magine it. He's talented. He's rich. He's famous. He's Kirk Douglas. And he's your dad. So how do you top that? How do you step out of the shadow cast by such a towering colossus – Spartacus no less – and make your own mark in the world which daddy dearest has dominated for decades?

It was a tough proposition and just imagine how easy it could have been for Michael Douglas to have either followed and then fallen in his father's giant footsteps, or worse still, taken the easy path and simply rode along on Kirk's substantial coat-tails. Instead, Michael Douglas has taken his father's legacy, built on it and now

MICHAEL DOUGLAS

A CHIP OFF THE OLD BLOCK

at the age of 60, he's created his own.

Douglas may have been a shaggy-haired member of a hippy commune in the Sixties but just like all the best laid-back, free-loving beatniks, he's gone on to blaze a formidable career, straddling two disciplines – acting and producing – like a man hellbent on success.

In a career that has spanned nearly 40 years so far, Douglas has produced a multitude of hit movies including the classic *One Flew Over The Cuckoo's Nest* (which garnered him an Oscar at the ripe old age of 31) and *The China Syndrome* through to box office smashes such as *Face/Off*.

His acting career has been equally successful – from the roguish hero in *Romancing The Stone* and his scenery chewing, Oscar-winning turn as Gordon Gekko in *Wall Street* through to his controversial roles as the disenfranchised D-Fens in *Falling Down* and the cheating hubby in *Fatal Attraction*, Douglas's roles show that he isn't afraid of putting himself on the line when up there on the big screen.

Indeed, if Tom Hanks is the everyman that every mother dreams her daughter will bring home for Thanksgiving, then Douglas's on-screen persona is that of the cynical, angry and edgy

A CHIP OFF THE OLD BLOCK

everyman that those very same mothers have warned their daughters about.

His characters, from Dan Gallagher in *Fatal Attraction* through to Det. Nick Curran in *Basic Instinct*, are angry, lust-filled hunter-gatherer types; in other words, they're a bit of a bastard really – not exactly the most PC of cinematic personas in a world where many A-list actors avoid such feisty roles for fear of tainting their perfectly manicured and pedicured on-screen images.

Perhaps Douglas's greatest gift as a producer and actor though, is his unerring ability to nail headline-grabbing issues just before they're about to happen or in some cases, generate debate because of the issues raised by his films.

The Douglas-produced and starred-in *The China Syndrome* tells the story of a nuclear power plant nearly going into meltdown, a theory that was scorned by experts on its release on 16 March 1979. Twelve days later though, the Three Mile Island nuclear plant spilled out radioactive gas into the surrounding area in America's worst nuclear accident – cue national debate and the film's box office takings shooting up into the stratosphere.

His immoral broker Gordon Gekko character in *Wall Street* also ensnared the public imagination

A CHIP OFF THE OLD BLOCK

especially since the stock market crash occurred just two months before its release; and *Fatal Attraction* ripped open the discussion on sexual politics, infidelity and promiscuity in a world that had been recently introduced to the horrors of HIV.

The controversy and intrigue surrounding Douglas's producing and acting career rages round his personal life as well. His difficult relationship with his father; his stay in a top clinic to combat his drinking problem; the breakdown of his first marriage; and his much publicised clash with the British media have all compounded to create the image of a man who's transformed himself from being the son of Hollywood legend Kirk Douglas, into Kirk Douglas being the father of Hollywood legend, Michael Douglas.

Add to this mix, there's also the small matter of his *Darling-Buds-Of-May*-to-December marriage in 2000 to Hollywood hot property (and one of Wales's finest exports) Catherine Zeta-Jones with whom he has two children. There may be exactly 25 years between them (they share the same birthday – 25 September) but if there is such a thing as royalty in Hollywood, then these two are it, attracting column inches by the truckload whether they're spending time in Hollywood or at

A CHIP OFF THE OLD BLOCK

their holiday retreat in Majorca; or hob-nobbing with the locals in Mumbles, Wales.

While Douglas's plans to star alongside his wife for the first time in the Stephen Frears-directed movie *MonkeyFace* have fallen through, it's only a matter of time before the couple end up sharing screen time together. All of which inevitably means that the shadow that Douglas's stature has been casting over the rest of Hollywood is set to expand ever further.

2

The grass is always greener

MICHAEL DOUGLAS

THE GRASS IS ALWAYS GREENER

Well, his pa must've been proud at least it's hard to imagine how Michael Douglas's mum felt when the school counsellor contacted her about her son. After all, it's not the typical problem a parent expects to deal with – they may worry that one day, no matter how well-behaved their pride and joy is, that their darlin' little un will get into trouble either for scrapping, truancy or being caught sniffing glue behind the vandalised bike sheds.

But for Diana Douglas, the mother of Michael Kirk Douglas, when Westport Junior High got in touch, it was the first sign that her first son was

THE GRASS IS ALWAYS GREENER

already on the way to becoming a sex symbol. According to the school counsellor, his presence at school was causing... problems.

Well, not through his own behaviour exactly but more through the actions of the female community at Westport Junior High in 1957. He was on the receiving end of "aggressive female attention," is how Diana Douglas recalled what the counsellor told her.

And he was only in his early teens. While most men reading this will sit there spitting nails in envy at the idea of Douglas already becoming something of a 'ladies' man' at such a sprightly age, it wasn't all silver spoons and cucumber sandwiches for the son of movie star Kirk Douglas.

So yes, he was on the way to becoming a young handsome man-about-town with a good education – and he wasn't exactly having money worries either. But it hadn't been an easy ride for the boy Douglas. In fact, his childhood reads like something out of an over-baked soap opera.

When Michael Kirk Douglas was born at 10.30am on 25 September 1944 at St Peter's Hospital in New Brunswick, he didn't arrive into a typical cosy pre-nuclear family unit – in fact, his father wasn't actually there when he eventually

THE GRASS IS ALWAYS GREENER

arrived because Kirk had acting commitments. All was decidedly not well between the couple anyway – to describe Kirk and Diana's time up until their marriage in 1943 as a whirlwind romance is the kind of understatement that would have Barbara Cartland spinning in her grave.

While Kirk Douglas and Diana Dill had first met at the American Academy of Dramatic Art in New York in 1939, they didn't date until much later. After a failed attempt to make it in Tinseltown (and after a brief dalliance with Errol Flynn no less), Diana returned to the Big Apple to carve out a career as a much sought-after model. In fact, it was a picture of her adorning the cover of *Life* magazine that caught seaman Kirk's eye who was now in the navy.

Obviously reminded just how drop-dead-gorgeous Diana was, Kirk quickly sent off a letter that would eventually lead to them spending two weeks together in New York while he was on leave. And by the end of the first day, Kirk had already asked Diana to marry him and on 2 November 1943, they tied the knot navy-style – under crossed swords in New Orleans.

An accident onboard the boat Kirk was serving on, though, saw his naval career come to a

THE GRASS IS ALWAYS GREENER

premature end and Kirk headed for the Big Apple to resume his acting career. By the time Michael K Douglas arrived, the dimple-chinned one had already landed his first steady job on Broadway in *Kiss And Tell*.

But a brand new bouncing baby (complete with that famed Kirk Douglas chin) couldn't help a marriage that was beginning to splinter. While Kirk Douglas was enjoying success both on Broadway and in Hollywood, his mood swings and hot-headedness coupled with his, let's say, 'flirtatious' nature with the ladies wasn't exactly helping the couple paper over the cracks either.

Kirk and Diana bought a house in California and Diana promptly fell pregnant again – Joel Andrew Douglas was born in 23 January 1947. Despite the new arrival, Diana and Kirk Douglas finally separated when she discovered that while she was away in New York, Kirk moved a lover into the California family home.

Perhaps unsurprisingly, their divorce was finalised on 8 February 1950 but as Michael Douglas stated later, it wasn't the soul-destroying experience some might've expected. His parents remain good friends and he feels that as long as children see both parents speaking amicably to

THE GRASS IS ALWAYS GREENER

each other, they don't have too many problems.

But Diana Douglas would put a mum's perspective on the events pointing out that "Michael especially felt a sense of loss. He was very, very angry with Kirk. A psychologist told me that Michael was shaken up badly in terms of who loved him and was there for him."

After the divorce, Diana and the two boys moved to New York where Michael started attending the Allen Stevenson School. It was here that the colossal form of his father's career first cast a shadow across Michael – he quickly became known as the son of a famous movie star because Kirk Douglas's turn in *Champion* thrust him into the Hollywood stratosphere.

Diana Douglas in the meantime was busy making a name for herself in theatre and TV. In 1951, Diana headed up to Ohio to play the lead in the play *Light Up The Sky*. Here she met fellow actor Bill Darrid and within two weeks of being together, they were already discussing marriage. In December 1956, they exchanged vows. In the meantime, Kirk Douglas had already remarried – this time to Anne Buydens in May 1954.

In 1995 Michael Douglas very nearly made his feature film debut. Kirk and Diana were shooting

THE GRASS IS ALWAYS GREENER

The Indian Fighter together in Oregon and Michael and Joel were given roles as two children who run, shouting, "The Indians are coming!" Their presumably outstanding performances, though, would ultimately end up being cut from the film.

Bill Darrid and Diana Douglas with Michael and Joel in tow moved to Westport, Connecticut in 1956. Kirk Douglas still figured large in his sons' lives and Michael was already beginning to respect his father's talent after he saw his dad playing Van Gogh in *Lust For Life*: "That's when I realised what a wonderful actor he is. I totally lost the reality that he was my father. Joel and I were immersed in the fact that he was Van Gogh, the artist; that's how persuasive a performance it was."

And the scene where Kirk cuts his ear off while looking into a mirror proved shocking for the two young lads: "(The way) the blood hit the mirror it was so real, we thought he'd cut his ear off."

When not watching his dad delivering overpowering performances on the big screen, Douglas exhibited the same traits for which he is so well-known – his dare-devil thrill-seeking. Climbing the highest trees, riding the fastest bikes and taking the kind of risks that would make

THE GRASS IS ALWAYS GREENER

grown men go bald overnight – in fact, Douglas once threw himself off a bridge and plummeted 70 feet into a fast-flowing river below.

It was during these times while he was attending Westport Junior High when Diana was informed by the school counsellor that Michael became 'victim' to "aggressive female attention." Indeed, so concerned was his mum about his effect on the opposite sex, she moved him to another school.

But that would be the least of the surprises in store for any dedicated follower of Michael Douglas's life.

3

The reluctant superstar

MICHAEL DOUGLAS

THE RELUCTANT SUPERSTAR

It's hard to imagine the rugged Michael Douglas as a hippy. After all, his on-screen persona means audiences know him as either a dark, edgy everyman character or as evil-incarnate such as Gordon Gekko in *Wall Street*. But back in the Sixties, Douglas sported a mammoth beard and was a fully signed up member of the flower power movement. How he got to this position is reflected by where he'd come from during his formative teenage years. One thing would link the transformation – women.

Although plagued by doubts that girls only liked him because of his movie-star father, this

THE RELUCTANT SUPERSTAR

didn't stop Douglas and his mates from the all-boys' school Choate, from making a beeline to nearby Yale to mingle with the fairer sex.

While the typical teenage behaviour continued, like it does for every young libido-driven male, being the son of a superstar meant that Douglas's vacations were perhaps somewhat more exotic than his peers. He regularly headed off to meet Kirk on the set of his latest film and invariably took on the role of general dogsbody on the likes of *Spartacus*.

Indeed, while working as an assistant film editor on *Lonely Are The Brave*, Douglas saw a slice of history being spliced together: "It's my favourite picture of my dad's," he confessed at the time, although his mind may have been elsewhere. Adding: "Down the hall from us, they were editing *Psycho*. And during lunch, we'd take our break sitting down there, watching outtakes of Janet Leigh in the shower scene. Going, 'OK, OK. Stop it there.'"

One might be excused for thinking that it was while working on *Lonely Are The Brave* and *Spartacus* that Michael Douglas decided he simply had to become an actor, but the truth is, at the age of 19, Michael Douglas didn't have a clue what he wanted to do – at one time, he even contemplated becoming a lawyer. By the time he graduated from Choate School, Michael Douglas dallied briefly with the idea of Yale, before deciding that there was only one real choice.

Going to the University of California probably had little to do with the educational possibilities and everything to do with the bikini babes – the ratio was rumoured to be three girls to every one boy after all – the miles of golden beaches and surfing featured in the university's prospectus. And what a prospect it must have seemed for Douglas as he packed his bags and headed to the West Coast to begin a new life on campus.

"It was great to be in California in the early Sixties," Douglas would recall later. "The UC system was in fabulous shape. The whole culture was just spectacular. It was an important time in my life and I think it paid off pretty well."

It was at university that Douglas would finally cut loose. Perhaps a little too much as it would turn out because he was eventually asked to take a leave of absence as he wasn't showing enough commitment to his English course.

Around the time of his partying at UCSB,

MICHAEL DOUGLAS

THE RELUCTANT SUPERSTAR

Douglas found himself leading the lifestyle of a full-blown hippy in the Sixties, moving into a hippie commune up in the hills above Santa Barbara in a region known as Mountain Drive. The free-lovin' and drug culture of the commune sent Hollywood's gossip columnists into overdrive – after all, here was the son of Spartacus shacked up with potheads, pill-poppers and other hedonistic types with a substantial population of "nekkid free-lovin' ladies".

By this time, Kirk Douglas was at the top of his game and wasn't exactly enamoured by Michael's stay at the commune. Despite living only 40 miles away from the commune, Kirk only visited his son once during his stay at Mountain Drive: "Well, he was living in this ramshackle building, at the top of these rickety steps," Kirk Douglas recalled, adding: "He slept on the floor. There was a box spring for me. I said, 'Next time I come to visit you, I'll stay in the Biltmore Hotel. I spent my life trying to get out of places like this.'"

As one columnist quipped about Kirk's reaction to his son's stay at the commune at the time: "If the kid had been in San Quentin he'd have had more visits!"

THE RELUCTANT SUPERSTAR

Now free of university for the foreseeable future, and for perhaps the first time in his life, Douglas found himself a 'proper job' – working at a petrol station in Westport.

For the son of a Hollywood star, one would have thought such tribulations were well beneath his stature, but Douglas threw himself into the job, swapping his silver spoon for an oily spanner. He has said that he drew genuine and immense satisfaction from being his "own man" as he drove tow-trucks and cleaned windscreens. And so much did he enjoy his job that he was awarded the heady honour of being made Mobil's Man Of The Month.

But Douglas found himself back on his father's sets soon enough. He was whisked off to the filming of *The Heroes Of Telemark* in Norway where as gopher, he found himself doing more menial work round the set.

Undeterred, he and his brother Joel went with their father to Israel to work on *Cast A Giant Shadow* where Michael would finally make his big screen debut playing a Jeep-wielding Israeli soldier.

Those times at the gas station and on the sets in Norway and Israel must have been important for Douglas – after all, he subsequently decided to return to university and threw himself into his studies; but with one major difference – this time he had his eye firmly set on the stage.

4

Back to New York

MICHAEL DOUGLAS

BACK TO NEW YORK

Kirk Douglas comment on his son's first proper role in front of a theatre audience in *As You Like It* was: "Michael was terrible". Harsh words indeed but so bad was his debut performance that Kirk Douglas decided pretty much then and there that the young buck didn't have what it took to become an actor.

In truth, Douglas's bumbling debut was probably more to do with his chronic stage fright at the time than anything else. And having Spartacus sitting in the audience judging you probably didn't help with the nerves either.

Douglas had settled back into uni life and

BACK TO NEW YORK

was pursing drama – he'd managed to evade being drafted for Vietnam war and while he is the first to admit that he wasn't proud of talking up an old football injury to avoid the draft, Douglas did strongly disagree with what was happening in Vietnam.

Such an attitude was typified by his am-dram anti-war antics. He and fellow wannabe thesps would 'shock' teachers and students alike when they stormed lectures and would then carry out a fake stabbing or shooting complete with bags of fake blood. One of the 'cast' would then deliver their message about the wrongs of the Vietnam war, then promptly leave, presumably scared that security might drag them off to the local cop show.

In the meantime, Douglas confounded his harshest critic – his dad – by leaving the *As You Like It* experience behind him and pulling off a blinding turn in *Escurial*. Both Kirk and Diana Douglas were transfixed by his performance of an old man; his mother didn't even realise it was him up there on stage at first. So impressed was Diana in fact, that she managed to get him an apprenticeship at the Eugene O'Neill Foundation Theatre in Waterford, Connecticut over the summer vacation.

MICHAEL DOUGLAS

BACK TO NEW YORK

While Douglas found himself helping with the actual construction of a new amphitheatre instead of playing Hamlet to packed houses, it was here that he met now life-long chum, Danny DeVito, who was a struggling young actor himself. When he graduated with his Bachelor Of Arts degree, Michael Douglas moved in with the diminutive wannabe-actor DeVito on his arrival in New York in 1968.

Things didn't start well though for Douglas in the Big Apple – while auditions were going well and he'd come too close to landing Broadway gigs, Douglas found himself being passed over at the last minute for someone else – for example, for the plays *Summertree* and *Saturday Adoption*. To add to this humiliation, if Douglas did land a role in a theatre or TV production, he wasn't even allowed to use his own name. Unfortunately, a successful TV chat host already had the exclusive rights to the name Michael Douglas, so the struggling actor became known as M.K. Douglas. This run of bad luck was topped off when Douglas landed a role in *City Scene*, an off-Broadway production only for it to close after just six performances.

Douglas had a minor breakthrough in 1969 in the shape of TV series *The Experiment*, in which he played a hippy, Wilson Evans, who struggles against the corporate system. The role put M.K. Douglas on the media map with critics picking over his performance, knowing full well that here was the son of the great Kirk Douglas. Fortunately, the reviews were positive – with one reviewer stating that Kirk's son could end up going all the way to the top – and shortly afterwards he landed a starring role in his first feature film, *Hail, Hero* playing Carl Dixon, a young pacifist who tries to win his father's respect by going to fight in Vietnam.

While *Hail, Hero* was not a box office hit by any stretch of the imagination, it did boost the young actor's profile and in 1970, he landed another lead role, this time in the drama *Adam At 6AM*. He played Adam Gaines, a young college professor who, tired of the cut and thrust of campus life, decides to spend his summer as a labourer in Missouri only to discover that the folk living out on the farms are frankly just as self-serving as the ones he left back in California.

The end result was hardly embraced by critics or the public but as well as offering an excellent opportunity for Douglas to learn more about film acting and production, *Adam At 6AM*

BACK TO NEW YORK

meant that the young Douglas had two pictures under his belt before his father Kirk cast him in the film version of *Summertree* in 1971.

Another movie with a strong anti-war theme, the cheery film opens on a dying soldier in Vietnam who recounts his life story – his battles with his parents, his sweetheart played Brenda Vaccaro and the happy days he spent at the summer tree. The film wasn't received well, but to be frank, it seemed like the press weren't interested anyway – they were far too busy banging out copy about Douglas's out-of-wedlock relationship with co-star Brenda Vaccaro with whom he shared homes in New York and California.

Douglas then went on to star in *Napoleon And Samantha* for Walt Disney Studios, a forgettable kids' flick in which two children, Jodie Foster and Johnny Whitaker turn to their friend Danny played by Douglas to help them keep a circus lion as a pet. Perhaps Douglas hoped that working on a big-budget-Disney production would further his film career but as it transpired, it actually marked the beginning of a six-year-absence from the big screen as the movie roles simply dried up.

Undeterred, Douglas headed back to New York where he landed the plum role of Jerry the

BACK TO NEW YORK

Naz in *Pinkville*, yet another anti-Vietnam play. His transformation from a young marine who finds the idea of killing repellent into a perfect killing machine by the end of the play finally garnered Douglas genuine critical success. The play was a hit, but more importantly, Douglas won a Theater World Award.

After *Pinkville*, Douglas headed for TV screens and found himself starring in a one-off episode of *Medical Center* as a psychiatric patient and in the hit series *The FBI* as a robber. It was this role that captured the attention of one of the most successful and influential men in America's TV industry at that time – Quinn Martin.

Martin had already carved his name as a producer who could deliver top series for America's networks during the Sixties and Seventies. After all, the actor-turned-producer was the man behind hits such as *The Fugitive*, *The Untouchables* and *The Invaders* and his latest project was bound to be another hit-in-waiting – a cop series called *The Streets Of San Francisco*.

5

Big in San Fran

MICHAEL DOUGLAS

BIG IN SAN FRAN

Douglas's turn as the gun-toting crook in *The FBI* caught Martin's eye and while veteran TV actor Karl Malden had already been cast as the hard-nosed (well, more brussel-sprout-nosed) detective Mike Stone, Martin still needed a young buck to play his wet-behind-the-ears partner, Steve Keller – and Michael Douglas fitted the bill perfectly.

The Streets Of San Francisco first aired in 1972 and, after a modest start, soon turned into another Quinn Martin success story. It also taught Michael Douglas a helluva lot about the production process and different stars and directors each week. This knowledge would prove indispensable in his movie-producing roles.

More importantly for Douglas, veteran actor Malden took Douglas under his wing and actively encouraged him to push himself and his character Kessler forward in the show: "Karl was incredibly generous and supportive," Douglas told *Cigar Aficionado Magazine* in 1998. "Up until that series, the second banana was always two steps back and in soft focus. He made sure that I really got the chance to shine. He was always saying, 'Come on, come on up here.'"

Any fears or naivety on his part disappeared as Douglas went on to do 104 hours of the show, sometimes shooting a whole episode in just seven working days; hitting 12 pages of dialogue every day. There would also be a different director each week and plenty of guest stars. Indeed, *The Streets Of San Francisco* saw other budding actors making their mark in one-off specials – Martin Sheen, Nick Nolte, Dean Stockwell, Don Johnson, Arnold Schwarzenegger and James Woods.

So comfortable did Douglas feel with his new production skills that he actually directed an episode guest starring Tom Selleck in 1975. Douglas also experienced critical success when he was nominated for a Golden Globe in 1975 for

MICHAEL DOUGLAS

BIG IN SAN FRAN

Best TV Actor in a drama role and then in 1976, an Emmy nomination for Outstanding Continuing Performance by a Supporting Actor. Couple all this with an annual pay packet well into the six-figure territory and starring in a show that attracted 30 million viewers a week, Michael Douglas had it made.

But despite all the success, things weren't all well. For starters, he was staying in San Francisco for eight months at a time, which understandably, was putting strain on his relationship with Brenda Vaccaro. The couple eventually split with Vaccaro stating that she found it "boring" with Douglas.

In a move though that would take the withering word "boring" and proverbially throw it in a bin marked "oh, really?", Michael Douglas handed in his notice after the series' fourth season. Douglas's exit saw his on-screen character bidding farewell to the rough and tumble world of crime fighting in San Francisco as he took on the rough and tumble world of teaching instead.

It wasn't the last time Douglas appeared in the show though – he made a special guest appearance in a two-hour made-for-TV movie *Back To The Streets Of San Francisco* in 1992. Well, sort of – he actually featured in Stone's dreams in a series of flashback clips from the original series. Perhaps the producers hoped that just using old footage of Douglas might bring some star-studded kudos to the TV movie. Who knows? But the proposed second TV movie was never made.

So what plans did Douglas have? Well, they were the kind that would take a TV celebrity adored by audiences across America and turn him into an international sensation.

6

Stepping out of Pa's shadow

MICHAEL DOUGLAS

STEPPING OUT OF PA'S SHADOW

You'd have to be insane. Unhinged. Deranged. Possibly bound for the funny farm, some would think. In fact, you'd have to be Michael Douglas. After all, it's not every day that you turn your back on a colossal pay cheque and a life riding on the coat-tails of your celebrity status. But Michael Douglas had fallen in love, head over heels in fact. Not with some diminutive starlet but with a book, *One Flew Over The Cuckoo's Nest* by Ken Kesey.

The book had practically become a member of the Douglas family household. While Michael had been interested in bringing it to the big screen since 1969, his father Kirk had been struggling to get the book up onto the silver screen for far, far longer. He'd already managed to get the book adapted into a play, and in 1963 took the lead part, Randle Patrick McMurphy, a con who pleads insanity to avoid work detail and then ends up in a mental asylum. There he raises hell among the inmates, challenging the system represented by the evil Nurse Ratched.

It was a bitter-sweet experience for Kirk. While the stage version had played to rapt audiences, the critics mauled its Broadway debut. Kirk decided that he'd show the cynics what for, by playing the larger-than-life character of McMurphy on-screen instead. And he subsequently spent years touting the script round Hollywood but to no avail.

Indeed, Kirk Douglas finally got to the stage of throwing in the towel and was about to put the film rights up for sale. It was then that a young man with absolutely zero producing-experience stepped in and stopped Kirk Douglas in his tracks – his son.

Michael had read the book at university and loved it because he saw it as the classic story of a man fighting the system. Off Douglas went to raise the budget but found himself heading down the same dead ends his father had. Undeterred, he rang round his dad's old contacts and came across Saul

STEPPING OUT OF PA'S SHADOW

Zaentz, the controller of Fantasy Records who promptly committed $2 million to the project and came onboard as Douglas's co-producer. The budget later swelled to $4 million, which for an independent movie in the Seventies was hardly insubstantial.

The next hurdle to clear was the screenplay adaptation itself – Zaentz wanted the book's original author, Ken Kesey, to have a crack at writing it but Kirk Douglas wasn't happy about this – he warned his son that they shouldn't hire the author because he was an unreliable character. Strong words perhaps, but as it would turn out, wise ones, as Kesey's draft turned out to be something of a mess in the eyes of Douglas and Zaentz. So they looked elsewhere for that perfect adaptation – which eventually ended up being written by Lawrence Hauben and Bo Goldman.

With a suitable screenplay in the bag, the producers turned their attention to finding the right director. As it turned out, Michael Douglas's first choice was Milos Forman, the Czech director who'd made the much-respected *Taking Off* in the States. Incredibly, it would transpire that Forman had also been Kirk Douglas's first choice when he was trying to get the picture off the ground.

Legend has it that Kirk approached Forman

in Prague in 1963 and offered him the job right there and then. On his return to the States, Kirk swiftly dispatched a copy of the book via post only for it never to arrive – it is believed that the document was seized by Czech customs.

Needless to say, Forman probably thought that Kirk had simply forgotten to post it but then, some 10 years later and after Forman had moved to America, he finally read *One Flew Over The Cuckoo's Nest*. His response to the subsequent job offer was a simple "yes" or to be more precise, "ya, ya, ya" – in fact, Forman stated that the book's portrayal of mental asylum culture reminded him of the communist country he had fled in 1968.

Then came a sticking point that could have derailed the entire production. Michael Douglas was on the search for a suitable actor to play the lead role of McMurphy. Trouble was Kirk Douglas always assumed that he'd play the con, but at the grand age of 60, he simply wasn't young enough to pull it off convincingly. As an understating Michael Douglas very diplomatically said: "I think my dad was disappointed that I hadn't given him the role."

With Kirk Douglas no longer in the running, various big names were approached – James Caan,

MICHAEL DOUGLAS

STEPPING OUT OF PA'S SHADOW

Gene Hackman, Marlon Brando and Burt Reynolds (who Forman was interested in for the part because of the star's "cheap charisma") but, for varying reasons – including Caan's misguided belief that the film simply wasn't visual enough – none of these actors were to play McMurphy. That honour would fall on Jack Nicholson who Douglas had seen as Billy 'Bad Ass' Buddusky in *The Last Detail*.

The hunt was then on to find an actress to play McMurphy's tormentor Nurse Ratched in what turned out to be one of cinema's most reviled characters. Michael Douglas later pointed out that it was almost impossible to find any female star who was willing to play Nurse Ratched because 'political correctness' meant that women simply weren't supposed to play the villain – especially one as spiteful and evil as the dreaded Ratched.

Jane Fonda, Anne Bancroft and Angela *'Murder She Wrote'* Lansbury were just some of the top-drawer actresses who turned their noses up at Nurse Ratched but perhaps such rejections – something that Michael Douglas had become used to when it came to anything involved with *One Flew Over The Cuckoo's Nest* – would ultimately prove to be good news for the production. His and Forman's casting of the sublime character actress

STEPPING OUT OF PA'S SHADOW

Louise Fletcher as Nurse Ratched was a genuinely inspired choice on their part.

After all, to have a big name actress on the billboard next to Jack Nicholson's name and sharing the big screen together may have actually diluted the tension between the two in the film. Fletcher's performance, like Nicholson's, added depth to a role that could so easily have been portrayed as an overblown pantomime baddy in the hands of the wrong actress.

With the rest of the cast slotting into place in the shape of Brad Dourif, Will Sampson, Scatman Crowthers and Douglas's buddy Danny DeVito, the film finally went into production. In what would become a typical trademark for Michael Douglas as a producer, there was no question of simply building the set of a mental asylum and then shooting it there. Nope, Douglas wanted to shoot in a real mental institution and one was finally found in Salem, Oregon – ironically, in the same town that features in the actual book.

It was a tough shoot not helped by the film's grim location and the fact that Douglas had decided on the "lunatics-running-the-asylum" approach to casting and crewing didn't make life any easier – after all, he let many of the asylum's real inmates take parts in the movie. As Douglas later pointed out, it meant some of Hollywood's finest cast and crew ended up working alongside convicted paedophiles, arsonists and murderers – a fact that Nicholson didn't pick up on when he first arrived on set, until Douglas explained why some of the actors weren't coming out of character when they broke for lunch.

To get away from such a claustrophobic set-up, Nicholson with a cast and crew posse in tow would hit the bars around Salem when the day's shooting had finished. But it wasn't all doom and gloom as Danny DeVito, who delivered a wicked turn as Martini in the movie, fondly recalled: "We were allowed to roam around those halls in that mental institution. We had the whole floor. We could dress in those costumes. We played 'foosball' (table football) and Pong, which was big at that time, and the only time we really came out of character was when Nicholson wanted to watch a ball game (his beloved Los Angeles Lakers). That kind of stuff is a joy."

Douglas summed up the experience of shooting *One Flew Over The Cuckoo's Nest* as a very close and intense one: "For the actors, it was emotionally exhausting," he recalled back in 1986: "Midway through the picture, we found out that one of our actors, Billy Redfield, the guy who played Harding-Hard-On was dying of leukemia. When he found out, he desperately wanted to finish this picture. He finished the picture and died six weeks later... So, yeah, it was intense."

Such intensity paid off though – the film was welcomed with open arms by audiences and critics alike at its premiere in 1975. Film critic Roger Ebert remembered that night well: "I was present at its world premiere, at the 1975 Chicago Film Festival, in the 3,000-seat Uptown Theater, and have never heard a more tumultuous reception for a film... After the screening, the young first-time co-producer, Michael Douglas, wandered the lobby in a daze."

In fact, film pundits the world over sang its praises back then and well into the future – *Empire Magazine* called it "a blistering attack on American society, that is at once exceptionally emotional and eternally uplifting," while *Box Office Magazine* wrote: "Dealing with insanity, *Cuckoo* qualifies as an experience many will feel deeply and pass on to others."

The son of Kirk Douglas had made his first movie and hit it big. Even better news followed in February, 1976 when the film picked up nine Oscar

STEPPING OUT OF PA'S SHADOW

nominations. While *One Flew Over The Cuckoo's Nest* faced some seriously stiff competition in the shape of Stanley Kubrick's *Barry Lyndon*, Sidney Lumet's *Dog Day Afternoon* and the film that had made everyone afraid of the water, *Jaws*, the small film about a man who takes on the establishment stormed home with five Oscars – Best Adapted Screenplay for Lawrence Hauben and Bo Goldman; a Best Director Oscar for Milos Forman; Best Actress for Louise Fletcher; Best Actor for Jack Nicholson; and of course Best Picture which meant that the 31-year-old-son of Kirk Douglas who had no track record of producing got his hands on his first (and by no means last) Oscar.

Kirk Douglas who was watching the Oscars at home was delighted: "When '*Cuckoo's Nest*' took five Oscars in 1976, including best picture, I was proud," he said, then quipped in the same interview that: "If I'd known what a big shot Michael was going to be, I would have been nicer to him when he was a kid."

The film's success on Oscar night saw the film re-released in cinemas across the US and the film ended up taking $112 million at the box office – and with five Oscars in the bag, Michael Douglas was no longer seen as merely the son of Kirk, but a Hollywood force in his own right.

And for Douglas himself, it meant it was party time as he and Jack Nicholson headed out on an international promotional tour of the world – rumours and speculation about just what they got up to while journeying between France, Sweden, Australia among other places, was the source of much media speculation.

Michael Douglas eventually drew a line under the rumour-mongering by telling the media that while he was on the promotional tour, he'd been single and therefore, like any red-blooded male of the species, had simply made the most of the situation "in the most decadent way."

But such hedonism was soon to end as Douglas's neglected heartstrings took over from his globe-trotting libido when he gazed across a crowded room, and looked straight into the eyes of the woman he was to marry.

7

One marriage and a meltdown

MICHAEL DOUGLAS

ONE MARRIAGE AND A MELTDOWN

Michael Douglas met his future wife on the most auspicious of occasions – at the Presidential inauguration of Jimmy Carter in January 1977. With Jack Nicholson and Warren Beatty in tow, the dapper Douglas attended the Pre-Inauguration Gala Concert and there, he laid eyes on a 19-year-old blonde-haired beauty, Diandra Luker, the daughter of a Spanish diplomat.

Wanting to make sure that neither Nicholson nor Beatty got the chance to go over and chat her up, he made a beeline for her and they instantly clicked. She was supposed to attend the next day's inauguration with a Congressman but blew him

ONE MARRIAGE AND A MELTDOWN

out to go with Douglas.

After the inauguration, they spent the day together at the Botanical Gardens. As it turned out, the movie hotshot was so love-struck with Diandra that he proposed to her just nine days after they'd met – and six weeks after that fateful meeting, they were wed. On 20 March 1977, they were married at Kirk Douglas's house and among the guests at the "low-key" wedding were Jack Nicholson, Warren Beatty, Gregory Peck and Karl Malden. To any pundit, Michael Douglas's whirlwind romance with Diandra Luker must have felt like Kirk Douglas's with Diana Dill. The question was would this Douglas marriage be more successful than the previous one?

In the meantime, Douglas was ready to return to work after his hedonistic promotional tour for *One Flew Over The Cuckoo's Nest* and his subsequent and sudden "settling down" with the woman of his dreams. Trouble was, well, there wasn't any.

While everyone else who had been involved in key positions on the film was fielding work left, right and centre, Douglas was left twiddling his thumbs. He finally realised that while actors and directors glean the benefits of an award-winning film in terms of career progression, a humble

ONE MARRIAGE AND A MELTDOWN

Oscar-winning wunderkind producer doesn't.

Such a realisation led Douglas to set up his own production company Big Stick Productions where began putting together a film that would show him as a man with his prophetic finger on the pulse of the day's big issues. Frighteningly prophetic, as it turned out when *The China Syndrome* finally hit the big screens.

Before that though, Douglas returned to the silver screen in an acting role after a break of six years – namely in the adaptation of the Robin Cook book *Coma* that tells the story of a young female doctor, Dr Susan Wheeler played by Genevieve Bujold, who starts to notice that seemingly healthy patients with routine medical complaints are dying after receiving treatment at the hospital where she interns.

Her off-duty investigations lead her to an institute where she discovers that the patients haven't died but have in fact been put into comas and their organs are then sold. Michael Douglas played her lover Dr Bellows who believes that there is certainly something mysterious about the patient's deaths but becomes increasingly convinced that Wheeler might just happen to be on the verge of a complete and utter nervous breakdown.

ONE MARRIAGE AND A MELTDOWN

It was a small and satisfying role for Douglas and perhaps a useful refresher course in the art of acting but the film's 1978 release was dwarfed by the arrival his first son, Cameron Mitchell Douglas, on 13 December. Professionally speaking, *Coma*'s story of cover-ups and evil conspiracies would also seem almost insignificant when Douglas' next film came out the following year – *The China Syndrome*.

The script, written by documentary-maker Mike Gray, had landed on the desk of Big Stick Productions back in 1976 and had immediately caught Douglas's attention. China Syndrome refers to the worst-case scenario of a nuclear reactor going into meltdown which would mean the failed reactor burning through the earth's crust and then popping out on the other side of the planet, in say China for example.

The film itself follows Kimberley Wells (played by Jane Fonda), a reporter who's more used to interviewing celebrities than covering major national events, as she sets out to do a fluff piece on the local nuclear power plant. She and her cameraman Richard Adams (played by Douglas) find themselves in the middle of an 'incident' that turns out to be the plant almost going into meltdown.

MICHAEL DOUGLAS

ONE MARRIAGE AND A MELTDOWN

Adams manages to shoot footage of the accident but the TV studio they work for refuses to show the report as officials tell the media that there is nothing to worry about. But plant engineer Jack Godell (played by Jack Lemmon) isn't so convinced and he and Wells begin to investigate what really happened with devastating consequences.

While the final film featured Jane Fonda's character Kimberley Wells, she didn't actually feature in Mike Gray's original script. It was in fact the cameraman who was to play the key character in the film who sets about exposing the cover-up. Richard Dreyfuss had been brought on board to play the role but had subsequently pulled out.

Douglas then contacted Jane Fonda about the film – herself no shrinking violet for taking on big issues in her personal life, never mind up on the silver screen. Fonda was still smarting from having failed to obtain the film rights to the Karen Silkwood story – the true life story of a woman working at a nuclear power plant who tried to inform journalists of her concerns about the site's safety but subsequently died under suspicious circumstances.

Fonda therefore was delighted with the script for *The China Syndrome* that covered similar

ONE MARRIAGE AND A MELTDOWN

themes and whistle-blowing issues. Well, she loved the script in principle at least. Before she would sign though, Fonda made it clear that there would have to be a couple of changes before she would commit to the project. First, Mike Grey who signed up to direct, would have to go – her concern was that his plans for a documentary style look to the film was a no-no in terms of creating a movie that must appeal to a wide audience. The Oscar-winning director James Bridges was drafted in instead.

But that change was nothing compared to her next stipulation – that a completely new main character be created for her which ended up being Kimberley Wells, the TV's on-air airhead, who uncovers the dastardly deeds of the plant's officials. Douglas would then take on the role of her cameraman. Though he had misgivings, Douglas agreed to the changes and the film finally went into production.

While the control room in the power plant featured in the finished film was perfectly recreated on a set, other interiors had to be shot at a utility company who had been told by the producers that the film wasn't a diatribe against the nuclear power industry. This white lie was finally exposed by a journalist who rather

ONE MARRIAGE AND A MELTDOWN

unhelpfully sent a copy of *The China Syndrome*'s shooting script to the workers at the plant.

Obviously, the workers at the facility were dismayed at the news and Jane Fonda who was already being touted by members of the press as a thoroughly bad egg because of her seemingly anti-patriotic views during the Vietnam war, found herself on the end of a stream of verbal abuse towards the end of the shoot.

Indeed, when she fractured her ankle during the last days of filming, it was reported that the facility's workers weren't exactly upset by the news. But any concerns that the film would damage the reputation of the nuclear power industry were unfounded – the industry did that all by themselves.

The China Syndrome was a massive hit on its release on 16 March 1979 – it was playing in 800 movie theatres across the country which in late-Seventies terms, was a 'maximum release'. Obviously the audiences found the idea of Jack Lemmon and Jane Fonda together on the big screen an enticing one, and the fact that Douglas and Columbia Pictures decided to market the movie as a top-drawer thriller instead of a film carrying an 'important message' about nuclear power proved a smart move.

As for the controversial content of the film, various well-heeled, supposed well-informed company-line-towing types from the nuclear industry were wheeled out in front of the media to denounce the film's portrayal of an accident at a power plant as the stuff of complete absurdity.

"Oops," is probably a distasteful understatement about what happened just 12 days later on Three Mile Island, Pennsylvania. At 4am on 28 March, the Unit 2 reactor in the island's nuclear power plant was closed because of human error. Exacerbated by more human and equipment cock-ups, the net result was that the reactor's core was left partially exposed, meaning that radioactive gas escaped into the surrounding area in what was America's worst nuclear accident.

Although the similarities of the events in both real life and in the film's fictional account were horrifying, Douglas and his team refused to draw comparisons for the press. He was worried that any comments might be misconstrued as trying to take advantage of the disaster to promote the film. "When the accident occurred, I got a phone call from Michael Douglas," recalled the film's co-writer Mike Gray to PBS's The American Experience

ONE MARRIAGE AND A MELTDOWN

series. He recalled what Douglas had said to him: "Look, whatever you do, don't answer any questions to the press. Our position is no comment. If we say anything about this, everybody's going to assume we're trying to take advantage of a disaster in order to sell this movie. And we don't want to be put in that position."

But their silence didn't stop the film becoming a runaway hit and while the nuclear disaster was thankfully contained, it gave Michael Douglas another home run in terms of his producing. With a mere two films under his belt, he was now labelled as one of the top producers in Hollywood.

8

When the going gets tough

MICHAEL DOUGLAS

WHEN THE GOING GETS TOUGH

W hile Michael Douglas might have been at the top of his game as a producer and glowing with success after Big Stick Productions signed a three-year-deal with Columbia, his acting career was dying on its feet – quite literally as it turns out when *Running* was released in 1979. Telling the jaded story of a deadbeat who turns into an Olympic Gold-winning marathon runner, Michael played the lead character Michael Andropolis.

While the toned Douglas certainly looked the part as the lean, mean, running machine that was Andropolis, the movie was poorly received by critics and audiences didn't exactly sprint to the

WHEN THE GOING GETS TOUGH

cinema to see it either – a fact reflected by its dire box office takings at the time.

Next came the romantic comedy *It's My Turn* where Douglas was cast as a baseball player who has to throw it all in because of an injury. While the film received a warmer response from critics than *Running*, again it was hardly the kind of success story that Douglas needed to launch himself as a Hollywood star. Indeed, it was all turning out to be a run of bad luck for Douglas – even his producing deal with Columbia was stagnating.

But there was some possible good news on the producing front for Douglas in the shape of the sci-fi project *Starman*, the tale of an alien who is stranded on earth and falls in love with a woman. To describe its journey to the big screen as somewhat tortured is an understatement – directors including Tony Scott, Michael Mann and Adrian Lyne all became involved with its production at various points but none lasted the course.

Starman ultimately ended up in the hands of John Carpenter who, in his eyes of fans at least, was something of a bizarre choice considering he was best known for directing nerve-shredding slasher flicks like *Halloween* and the classic paranoia-fest that was *The Thing*. But as is the

WHEN THE GOING GETS TOUGH

way with Carpenter (when he's on form at least), he turned in a memorable and, in the case of *Starman*, touching picture with Jeff Bridges playing the alien who falls head over heels for Karen Allen.

Unfortunately, when the film was eventually released in 1984, it walked out straight into a world of hurt. The major stumbling block was not the film itself but another one about a cute 'ickle alien called *E.T. – The Extra Terrestrial*. Directed by Steven Spielberg who was already a colossus among directors, *E.T.* was a huge hit at the box office. While *Starman* fared well at the box office, audiences saw it as a poor man's *E.T.* To add insult to injury, the film's backers Columbia had actually turned down *E.T.* to make *Starman* instead.

While perhaps if he had foreseen *Starman*'s eventual outcome he would have baulked at going with it, Michael Douglas was already experiencing tough times. The glow of success that he had enjoyed with both *One Flew Over The Cuckoo's Nest* and *The China Syndrome* was beginning to stutter and his acting career had also been put on hold after a skiing accident left Douglas shacked up at home for several months with Diandra, Cameron and a one helluva nasty blood infection.

In 1983, Douglas returned to the big screen

WHEN THE GOING GETS TOUGH

after a three-year gap in the thriller *The Star Chamber*. Playing a disillusioned Superior Court Judge Steven Hardin, he is approached by The Group, a shadowy organisation of senior judges, who initiate Douglas's character into their ranks. They operate above the law by passing secret sentencing on criminals who are then given vigilante-style punishments.

Of course, it all goes horribly wrong when The Group gets one of its sentences wrong and 'convicts' an innocent man. Hardin then tries to expose them but finds himself on the run from a hit-man hired by The Group. Unfortunately, for the third time in a row, another Douglas-starring film proved to be a disappointment at the box office – it was becoming increasingly clear that Douglas the actor – and to a lesser extent, the producer – was in need of a hit.

And it was a waitress who offered it to him on a plate in the shape of *Romancing The Stone*. Budding author Diane Thomas wrote the script about a romance novelist, Joan Wilder, who journeys to Columbia to rescue her kidnapped sister where she meets the cad, Jack Colton. The swash-buckling, high-adventure script crossed Douglas's desk and on reading it, he handed waitress Diana Thomas the biggest tip of her life in the form of a cheque for $250,000.

Kathleen Turner, who had turned in a steamy performance in the thriller *Body Heat* signed up for the role of Joan Wilder but a succession of major stars baulked at playing Jack Colton, Wilder's eventual lover. The main problem was that the image-conscious celebs knew the film was Joan Wilder's, not Colton's. Faced with such reluctance, Douglas took on the role himself.

Douglas's buddy Danny DeVito was then brought on board as the diminutive chap who chases Wilder and Colton across Columbia. The Robert Zemeckis-directed shoot itself was gruelling – shot in Mexico, the cast and crew were deluged by rain that swept away roads and locations. In what would lead cast members to rename Mexico 'Douglasland', Michael Douglas drafted in gravel carrying trucks that would ride into action whenever a road was needed to access a particular location.

There were other far more serious incidents – an alligator wrangler had his hand bitten off, while an errant boulder would have wiped out the crew if it had started its roll down a mountain five minutes earlier. As it was, the runaway rock managed to break one man's leg, another's arm

WHEN THE GOING GETS TOUGH

and scar Kathleen Turner's knee.

But for all the melodrama on set, the $10-million-movie turned into a $100 million plus hit at the box office. At last, Douglas had an out-and-out populist hit under his belt – and one in which he had starred. The film's studio Twentieth Century Fox was understandably delighted with the movie. In fact, so happy were they at the sight of their bank coffers filling that they wanted a sequel. And pretty damn sharpish as well – only 18 months after *Romancing The Stone* had hit the silver screen.

While it was normal practice for Douglas to produce and star in the same movie, this period saw him doing the same – but on two different pictures. He was actor and producer of the *Romancing The Stone* sequel, *The Jewel Of The Nile*, and also an actor playing Zach in Richard Attenborough's big screen adaptation of the iconic musical *A Chorus Line*.

A schedule clash meant that in a display of multi-tasking even Bill Gates would be proud of, Douglas actually set up his *Jewel Of The Nile* production office in his *A Chorus Line* dressing room at the Mark Hellinger Theater where he set to work hiring suitable writers to come up with a good enough script for the continuing adventures

WHEN THE GOING GETS TOUGH

of Joan and Jack – it wasn't easy because the first film's writer Diane Thomas was now working for Steven Spielberg.

More disappointment would eventually follow courtesy of Spielberg as *Romancing The Stone*'s original director, Robert Zemeckis, was busy working on *Back To The Future.* Instead the director of *Alligator*, Lewis Teague, stepped in to direct the movie.

Undeterred by the setbacks, Douglas drafted in Lawrence Konner and Marc Rosenthal to work on the new screenplay and following his brief, they turned in a first draft which showed that while Joan and Jack may have been living in luxury, they were bored with their lives. After hearing about the jewel of the Nile, they head for Sudan and discover that the jewel in question is in fact... err... a spiritual guru actually. Of course the dimwitted Danny DeVito character Ralph was also back onboard who once he gets whiff of this 'fabled' jewel, heads off after Joan and Jack.

The film was to be shot in Morocco – perhaps it was because Douglas was still in New York working on *A Chorus Line* so couldn't oversee the sequel's pre-production that things weren't going to plan. Douglas needed a reliable and trusted pair of hands to work alongside him, so Joel Douglas flew over and together the brothers began cracking heads, pulling locations together and hiring and perhaps more importantly, firing all the right people. While the production was back on course, the film though quickly became seen as cursed.

The production designer, location manager and unit pilot were all killed in a plane crash while on a location scout over the Atlas Mountains. Then Kathleen Turner decided that she didn't like *Jewel Of The Nile*'s script claiming that without a female screenwriter, her character had simply been reduced to a stereotype. After Douglas tried diplomacy, it would eventually take the menace of a $25 million lawsuit to bring Turner back onboard, plus a swift piece of script-doctoring on Diane Thomas's part to allay any fears Turner had about Joan's character.

Matters on the film's production didn't improve though – there was a crew uproar when they were forced to double-up in their accommodation while on location; the row was 'resolved' when Douglas, casting off his congenial manner, fired the trouble-makers. Then a key set was constructed and promptly swept away by floods. Illnesses such as dysentery, cholera and malaria also ran rampant

WHEN THE GOING GETS TOUGH

through the production and it must have been a relief for all concerned when the shoot finally wrapped.

Douglas later described making the movie as "a war" but in December 1985, *The Jewel Of The Nile* became a box office smash (with a hit theme song by Billy Ocean featuring Douglas, Turner and DeVito in the video), even if the critics weren't so enamoured of the finished film as they were with *Romancing The Stone*.

Unfortunately, the press's pen-wielders were positively hateful about *A Chorus Line* that was released in the same month. But for Douglas at least, his credentials as potential leading man material had now received an official stamp of approval from the people who really counted – the ticket-buying public – and his next film would establish him forever in the minds of audiences worldwide as a true star.

Michael Douglas as Steve Keller in 'The Streets of San Francisco'. Starring alongside Karl Malden, the show first aired in 1972. After a modest start it was a hit and at its peak was attracting 30 million viewers a week.

*Michael Douglas in a scene from 'Basic Instinct' (1991) pictured
with Sharon Stone. Douglas plays homicide detective Nick Curran
who is investigating the death of a rock producer. The prime
suspect is the producer's buddy Catherine Tramell (Sharon Stone*

*Michael Douglas and Catherine Zeta-Jones married in
New York in 2000. They have two children Dylan (born 2000)
and Carys (born 2003).*

Douglas's career has spanned more than 40 years as actor and producer in numerous award-winning films, including: 'One Flew Over the Cuckoo's nest', 'Romancing the Stone', 'Wall Street' and 'Traffic'.

9

The wonder boy

MICHAEL DOUGLAS

THE WONDER BOY

The term 'bunny boiler' is common slang now in the twenty-first century for someone, normally female, who's idea of love and dating is bordering on the psychotic. For the Western world over, it perfectly encapsulates an unhinged lover all because of one scene in a film that would storm the box office back in 1987 – *Fatal Attraction*.

On the face of it, the story's a simple one – Dan Gallagher, lawyer and "happily married man" with one child, decides to "play away" one weekend while his wife and child are visiting her parents. The object of his midlife crisis is Alex Forrest played by the frizzy-haired Glenn Close. What he thought

THE WONDER BOY

would be a couple of steamy sessions of nookie turn into every cheating hubby's worst nightmare when Alex falls pregnant and then starts demanding he takes responsibility.

Cue much scenery chewing as Douglas's character refuses to help her which all culminates in the classic scene where Mrs Gallagher finds the daughter's bunny happily bubbling away in a pot. Unskinned of course. By the end of the film, the spurned woman Alex had turned into the knife-wielding bunny-boiling maniac who had more in common with Jason from *Friday the 13th* than the career-driven and lonely businesswoman seen during the rest of the movie.

While *Fatal Attraction* became one of the iconic films of the Eighties, it came so close to never being made. Why? Because the script scared the living hell out of Hollywood execs. The main character's an adulterer, they squealed. After all, here's a man who sleeps with a relative stranger in the opening act of the film – even though Dan's married to the perfect wife (played by Anne Archer). And Dan has the perfect all-American daughter to bring up as well. He's a bona fide all-American family man. Who cheats with a woman who's been on the wrong end of a set of curling

THE WONDER BOY

tongs one too many times. What a complete and utter scumbag.

And just who could play a cheating husband with the right degree of sympathy so that audiences would actually feel for him as his life fell to pieces around him? Well, Michael Douglas of course, in a role that would define his everyman character with a fatalistic side that he would build on in future films such as *Basic Instinct* and *Disclosure*.

It was actually producers Stanley Jaffe and Sherry Lansing who realised Douglas was the perfect actor to play Dan Gallagher. Lansing in particular had already noticed his professionalism and charisma while working with him on *The Star Chamber*. Douglas in the meantime had been plugging his own 'man-who-has-it-all-is-brought-down-by-his-own-todger' screenplay *Virgin Kisses* but would eventually pass on it to play the lead in *Fatal Attraction*.

Not that it was easy honing the screenplay down into the finished product – Douglas and the team would regularly rewrite parts of the script to ensure that the audience wouldn't simply turn off. Getting the balance right between Dan's extra-curricular sexual activity and how he and his family end up being punished by the deranged

THE WONDER BOY

Alex was a tough proposition. In fact, they ended up with several different endings that were eventually whittled down to just two.

The first (which incidentally was released in Japan among other areas and went down equally well) sees Glenn Close's character killing herself with a kitchen knife – only trouble being that Dan's prints are all over it so he's sent down for her 'murder'. The other (the one we all know and most of us love) ends up with Close going mental with said kitchen knife in the Gallagher's family home which ends up with her being splattered all over the bathroom wall.

Well, audiences must have loved this ending because, in the expert hands of director Adrian Lyne and with a cast all delivering the goods (Close and Archer were both Oscar-nominated for their performances), the film not only took the box office by storm, it devoured it – the $14-million-film took over $200 million worldwide by the time its run had finished at the box office and video shops. It also consumed the media – there were a multitude of objections to the film – mainly that the portrayal of Dan's unprotected sexual antics were wholly irresponsible in a world recently introduced to the horrors of AIDS (gee, a struggle with a condom would've worked so well in that sizzling elevator scene, right?); that Alex's transformation into a nutcase was an affront on womankind; that the sex scenes were too explicit. And so on.

But somewhere in the outbursts of political correctness (and among hacks desperately looking for something to fill their columns), audiences lapped the film up as couples piled into the cinemas to watch *Fatal Attraction.* And would then afterwards argue about who was the worst out of Dan and Alex.

But perhaps for all the discussion and controversy though, *Fatal Attraction* can be seen as no more than a glossy *Friday the 13th* or *Halloween,* with its key message the same as so many slasher movies of that era – if you're bad (i.e. have nookie out of wedlock) then you'll end up on the wrong end of a very large kitchen knife.

Chin-stroking aside, more importantly for Douglas though was that it put him well and truly on the path to superstardom – and not for playing a muscle-bound meathead like so many of his peers but for playing an everyman with a difference – one with a frustrated dark side. Men the world over could relate to this guy because of his faults –

THE WONDER BOY

instead of simply wanting to be a pumped-up kebab spit on legs packing an Uzi, a six pack and a matching set of comedy biceps.

Of equal importance was that *Fatal Attraction* would further underline Douglas's unerring ability to catch the mood of the public at the time, as he would with his next film. For followers of Douglas's career, it comes as no surprise that instead of jumping on the leading man bandwagon straight after *Fatal Attraction* and preening his on-screen persona in to something decidedly more cuddly and approachable, Michael Douglas would then go on to steal an entire film in which his character didn't just boast a dark side. He was the dark side. Of the red brace-wearing, limousine-riding corporate culture of America.

That film was, of course, *Wall Street* that saw Douglas taking on the iconic character Gordon Gekko in Oliver Stone's diatribe of the world's most powerful financial base. Stone cast Douglas because "I figured, he knows money," he said. "He knows that world – use it." He also found the idea of using Douglas appealing because he thought it would really break the Michael Douglas mould: "I thought that to take Mike, who is sort of the übersoft, and make him into a Wall Street sharpie,

THE WONDER BOY

was an interesting innovation."

And Gekko was a character that would also flex Douglas's acting skills as he and Oliver Stone clashed on set as the director felt Douglas could sometimes be "lazy" as a performer, or perhaps just too damn "übersoft" for Stone's liking. Douglas later revealed just how punishing a master Stone could be: "Oliver Stone early in the film came in my trailer one day and said: "Are you okay?" I said: "Yeah, I'm fine" [He asked] "You doing drugs?" I said: "No, I'm not doing drugs, no!" He said: "Because you look like you never acted before in your life."

Understandably somewhat perturbed by his director's take on his work, Douglas high tailed it to the dailies screening room to watch the latest reels of his performance, only to find that they were 'pretty good' as he would later tell Stone who then would reply: "Not bad, is it." I said, "What are you doing?"… [it turned out that] Stone wanted just a little more 'oomph'. What he did for me was push the buttons and wasn't afraid to be adversarial."

Indeed, so successful was Douglas's incarnation of Gekko that the character came to symbolise all that was wrong in the corporate world and generated a grudging and perhaps secret nod of respect from

THE WONDER BOY

audiences as he audaciously shafts people from one deal to the next, showing no remorse or regret. The 'greed is good' speech became an oft-quoted classic scene – and such scenes would see Douglas working with a speech coach to control his breathing and the character's inflections.

On its release, *Wall Street*, like *Fatal Attraction* and *The China Syndrome* before it, scored yet another home run in terms of timeliness. After all, just weeks before, Wall Street had experienced Black Monday where investors had lost millions on the stock market through the insidious actions of people just like Gekko.

Douglas's turn as Gekko also gave him his second Oscar – this time for Best Actor in 1988. As Douglas told *The Orange County Register*: "That was the moment when I became my own man. That was the moment when I was no longer a second generation. I was no longer Kirk Douglas' son…"

While Douglas went on to set up a new three-year deal with Columbia and began producing duties on two new films from his Big Stick Productions company in the form of *Flatliners* and *Radio Flyers*, it wasn't long before Douglas was back in front of the camera.

While the public was now used to seeing

MICHAEL DOUGLAS

THE WONDER BOY

Douglas play a guy with issues, they probably weren't expecting Nick Conklin, a New York cop who's happy to take backhanders, is under investigation by internal affairs and on his days off, takes part in illegal motorbike racing. Sporting a hairdo just a few inches short of a mullet plus a stinky-looking set of biking leathers, Conklin is, to be blunt, a thoroughly typical Eighties' caricature of a 'man on the edge'.

This character is thrust into the Japanese underworld when he and his partner Charlie (played by Andy Garcia) escort Japanese Mafioso Sato back to Tokyo's authorities and inadvertently hand him over to his men dressed as Japanese cops. Conklin's determination to get Sato back in custody results in Charlie's death at the hands (and swords) of Sato's (strangely unthreatening-looking) biker gang. Conklin then teams up with Japanese cop Masahiro Matsumoto to bring in the bad guys, while 'riffing' on each other's different cultural backgrounds.

With Ridley Scott onboard to direct, it had all the makings of a surefire hit and the role of Conklin must have appealed to Douglas's love of characters carrying enough emotional baggage to fill the cargo hold of a Boeing 747 – but on *Black*

THE WONDER BOY

Rain's release, some people took offence to Conklin's borderline xenophobic/racist attitudes towards his Japanese peers.

Yet others simply looked at Conklin's 'cop on edge' image (including obligatory ciggies, motorbike and reflective sunglasses) and remarked how he looked like a bloke suffering from an acutely obvious (and embarrassing) 'mid-life crisis' and who, more importantly, really needed to take a shower.

The film opened on 24 September 1989, and drummed up moderate business at the box office. Thankfully his next film – that hit the screens three months later – saw Douglas team up with Kathleen Turner and Danny DeVito again. Not in another *Romancing The Stone* sequel, but in the DeVito-helmed jet-black comedy *The War Of The Roses*. Yet again when it comes to Douglas's choice of films, the movie's premise was the kind that would've had Hollywood execs reaching for their beta-blockers; for once, a film's tagline perfectly summed up the film it was hawking: "Once in a lifetime comes a motion picture that makes you feel like falling in love all over again. This is not that movie."

Based on the book by Warren Alder, *The War Of The Roses* tells the story of successful lawyer Oliver Rose and his seemingly perfect wife and homemaker, Barbara, who find themselves at each other's throats when they realise they can't stand each other. Told through the words of their divorce lawyer played by DeVito, the film is no po-faced, hand-wringing drama but a dark portrayal of their increasingly hilarious attempts to split their house and worldly goods up. This leads to the outbreak of marital war – witness Oliver Rose unloading his bladder over Barbara's gourmet cuisine and Barbara trashing his vintage sportscar with a monster pick-up.

Sensationally (for a mainstream Hollywood movie with a $30 million budget – still large in 1989), the end saw both characters die as they fought to the bitter end, culminating in the couple being stranded high up on a chandelier. As well as being a surprising and more importantly satisfying ending, it also meant that the director (and prankster) DeVito found himself in a situation that he was delighted to exploit. When shooting the scene he called for lunch, leaving the two stars dangling 40 feet up in the air – sweet revenge for the hellish shoots of *Romancing The Stone* and *The Jewel Of The Nile*: "I used to say 'Remember the jungles, Michael? Remember the desert heat? Remember the donkeys and camels?"

recalled a joking DeVito.

Despite the film's success, it generated a very healthy $84 million on its release, Douglas decided that he needed to take it easy and spend some serious time with wife Diandra and son Cameron. And what the heck, after all, the Douglas-produced *Flatliners* had racked up over $60 million at the US box office so he could afford to take some time out. Perhaps more importantly, he needed some quality time in front of the telly – flicking through the various sport channels instead of the movie channels. As he has famously stated, he prefers sports to movies as you never know how they are going to end.

After his 18 months playing the ideal husband and father, Douglas returned to the big screen once more, this time in *Shining Through* alongside Melanie Griffith, about a secretary sent to Berlin in World War Two by her boss to spy on a high-ranking German. Perhaps yearning for the days of playing Jack Colton in *Romancing The Stone* and *Jewel Of The Nile*, Douglas wanted to play a the heroic chap who saves the damsel in distress and not be responsible for carrying the picture.

What he actually ended up with was a box office failure that was ridiculed by critics mainly

THE WONDER BOY

because of Melanie Griffith's miscasting in the role of Linda Voss. If Douglas had been worried about losing that all-important winning streak and ability to latch onto controversial issues, he needn't be – all hell was about to break loose in a film that would appeal to everyone's baser instinct.

10

A head for trouble

A HEAD FOR TROUBLE

Being surrounded by 50 members of the San Francisco Police Department's riot police probably wasn't what Michael Douglas and his fellow cast members had in mind when the thriller *Basic Instinct* started shooting. The reason for the armed escort on every location shoot was because extremists within the city's gay community were extremely hacked off with his next feature, *Basic Instinct*. To understand why, one has to go back to the script.

Penned by Hollywood über screenwriter Joe Eszterhas, the script was bought by Carolco Pictures for a princely sum of $3 million and told the story of

A HEAD FOR TROUBLE

homicide detective, Nick Curran, investigating the death of a rock producer who's been stabbed 35 times with an ice pick. All on the cusp of an orgasm as it turns out. Enter the prime suspect – blonde bombshell and the producer's bonk-buddy Catherine Tramell (played by Sharon Stone) who drags Curran into a world of sex, lies and cocaine.

The price for the script was a record-breaker at the time and as part of the deal, Eszterhas insisted that Irwin Winkler, producer of *Raging Bull* be brought on board to handle the film. In return, Carolco Pictures drafted in Michael Douglas in the lead role and Paul Verhoeven, a director already known for controversy bating movies such as *RoboCop*.

Things started to go wrong almost immediately, Verhoeven, showing his usual flair for the inflammatory, desperately wanted to include an erect penis in what would have been something of a first for a mainstream Hollywood flick. Plus he wanted a full-blown lesbian scene in the film. In the meantime, Douglas wasn't happy with his character always playing second fiddle to Stone's character – that she always seemed to be calling the shots while he scurried round after her like a sexually-frustrated Yorkshire Terrier.

MICHAEL DOUGLAS

A HEAD FOR TROUBLE

The whole situation ultimately proved too much for Eszterhas and Winkler who subsequently walked out, leaving Verhoeven to work on a new version of the script while Douglas headed off to Europe to shoot *Shining Through*. On his return though, Douglas discovered that the director had thrown in the towel on the various rewrites and had gone back to Eszterhas's original script.

Verhoeven also made up with Eszterhas who was brought back onboard. By now though, the script's storyline had slipped into the public domain and sectors of the gay community (and women's groups) were horrified at the film's premise, labelling it homophobic, misogynistic and even bi-phobic.

Eszterhas in the meantime decided – at the request/demands of protesters – that it would be better if Douglas's character was replaced by a lesbian. On this occasion though, Verhoeven wasn't budging an inch and shooting finally began – which led to the SFPD's finest being drafted in to protect location shoots after one property owner (a gay activist himself) received death threats from outraged non-heterosexuals.

The shoot was also difficult for other reasons – namely the film's notorious sex scenes which

A HEAD FOR TROUBLE

featured Douglas and Stone indulging in steamy sex sessions. While Verhoeven would quite happily have shown everything up there on the big screen, the picture's backers were insistent that the film's sex scenes be pared down enough to avoid getting an NC-17 rating. To appease the censors, Verhoeven ended up snipping 42 seconds of 'too-hot-to-handle' material from the US release of the movie.

"The sex is all choreographed," Douglas pointed out after people started to wonder if Douglas and Stone had simply 'gone for it' because the sex scenes were so realistic. He explained that every act is talked through before filming and that it is eventually broken down into beats, so that each actor knows what is going to happen next.

Indeed, things became so rehearsed and relaxed for Douglas and Stone that when photographer Firooz Zahedi turned up to take official snaps of the sex scene, he started taking photos as Douglas talked him through the sex scene while he casually went through the motions of what would eventually end up on the big screen. This included Douglas pulling up Stone's skirt to reveal she was wearing nothing underneath. As Zahedi recalled in 1995: "I notice my assistant has gone pale, but I keep

A HEAD FOR TROUBLE

shooting. I sent the photos right to TriStar; I was worried someone would steal them. Later we reshot tamer versions, which the studio used. But one day I got a copy of an Italian magazine and on the cover was my shot of Michael. With his head buried in her doody!"

While Douglas and Stone may have been comfortable with the saucy scenes, Verhoeven wasn't having such a good time. At one point, the trails of production – and clashes with Douglas – proved so much for the Dutch director that he was carted off to hospital with an unstoppable nose bleed which meant that filming was stopped for a few days. Once the film finally hit the screens, the negative publicity didn't affect the film's popularity. While protesters gathered in force outside its premiere in LA, the film went on to make nearly $120 at the US box office alone.

Casting an eye back to the Eighties from the more cynical twenty-first century, one has to wonder what all the fuss was about – after all, there's no hate-filled vat of acid at the heart of *Basic Instinct*. The finished film is a cheesy, popcorn-munching adult crowd-pleaser.

Yes, the questionable violence of Curran's rough sex session with Jeanne Tripplehorn's

A HEAD FOR TROUBLE

character still raises an eyebrow but as for the rest – well, it features sex; violence; death by ice pick; car chases; women indulging in lipstick lesbianism (something that may have been contentious back then but now seems old hat in the days of *Sex And The City*); and most importantly for male members of the audience, Sharon Stone's erogenous zones. For females, it doesn't feature any frontal shots of Douglas's manhood but it does show off his (admittedly pert) bottom.

If Douglas felt battered by the protesters at the time, he showed no signs that it would affect his movie role choices in the future. He went from outraging gays and women with *Basic Instinct* and into fresh protests from defence workers and minority groups when *Falling Down* hit the screens.

Telling the story of a nameless laid-off defence employee D-Fens (his car's number plate), the divorcee who wants to see his daughter on her birthday, finally snaps in an LA traffic jam and unleashes his pent-up rage on anyone who crosses his path on that fateful summer's day. He turns into a one-man wave of violence and chaos who rapidly escalates from trashing a convenience store because of the price of coke to using a rocket launcher. Hot on his tail, is the soon-to-retire

A HEAD FOR TROUBLE

veteran cop Prendergast played by Robert Duvall who finally tracks him down, leading to a confrontation on a pier where D-Fens, finding himself on the wrong end of a gun, asks: "I'm the bad guy?" before being blown away.

From such a premise, it's perhaps not so surprising that every major Hollywood studio said no to the idea of actually making a movie where there was no real good or bad guy. Indeed, the film's producer Arnold Kopelson was all set to make it for cable TV until Douglas read the script and decided that *Falling Down* was one of the best scripts he'd ever come across.

With Douglas onboard (and after wranglings about his salary with the film's backers Warner Bros) and director Joel Schumacher signing on for helming duties, the film's shooting must have been a 'breeze' compared to *Basic Instinct*. Sporting a buzz cut, a shirt pocket full of pens and a pair of glasses that looked like they were fashioned in the Fifties, Douglas looked like the cartoon character Dilbert armed with an Uzi. It was hardly the most flattering of looks but, as anyone knows by this point, Douglas isn't one for taking on acting roles based on his vanity.

On its release, the media went into overdrive

with the film making front page news; after all, the content was extremely close to the bone after various incidents where people had gone 'postal' in their local burger joints. Defence workers were making their presence felt as well because they were just a tad worried that they'd all be branded by the public as maniacs just waiting for the wrong traffic jam before heading out on to the streets to dish out some D-Fens-style 'justice'.

But as Douglas would say about D-Fens's character: "A lot of people are angry out there now. They've worked hard all their lives and they've got nothing to show for it. But they don't know who to be angry at."

While Douglas later said that the role of D-Fens in *Falling Down* was the greatest acting performance of his career, in only a matter of months, Douglas the man had his own falling down when he booked himself in to the Sierra Tucson clinic in Arizona at the end of 1992. British tabloids began to pump out rumours that he was being treated for sex addiction, something that Douglas himself would furiously deny: "I want to make this really clear," he said in 1995. "There was a lot of tabloid journalism about my supposed sex addiction. Bullshit. It's all bullshit.

A HEAD FOR TROUBLE

That was a good story, but not the issue for me...
I mean, come on, I never pretended to be a saint.
But give me a break."

He admitted the real reason he checked in
was for substance abuse, chiefly alcohol problems.
And the fact he had been burning the candle at
both ends for too long. Scratch further beneath the
surface though and it wouldn't be obtuse to say
that the death of his stepfather earlier in the year
coupled with a marriage that was going through a
bad time because of Douglas's time away shooting
films all over the world, probably all contributed
to his decline and subsequent stay at the Sierra
Tucson clinic.

It was two years before Douglas appeared on
the big screen again – this time in the big screen
adaptation of Michael Crichton's best-selling
book, *Disclosure*. And while he may have been
away dealing with his personal problems, there
was absolutely no change when it came to his
sixth sense at being able to choose controversy-
bating material. The story revolves round Tom
Sanders, a top software engineer at a Seattle
company who goes to work one morning only to
discover that an ex-girlfriend, Meredith Johnson
(played by Demi Moore) has landed the plum job

he thought he was in the running for.

In a typical Crichton role reversal, Meredith makes advances on Sanders, who spurns them which results in Johnson trashing his reputation and our hapless hero finding himself in the middle of a sexual harassment complaint. Such a premise was backed-up with the usual solid soundbites from Douglas himself as he pondered what a woman wants in a man. He claimed that while women say they want an 'understanding' man, they are attracted to 'dominating' ones.

Of course, any Douglas film hitting the screens from this era invariably meant someone, somewhere getting their placards out and taking to the streets – in the case of *Disclosure* (like *Fatal Attraction* and *Basic Instinct* before it), it was feminists who weren't happy. And their objection? Well, it seemed that they were unhappy that Demi Moore's character was being portrayed as the 'bad guy'.

Whether such outrage could be viewed as justifiable opinion or simply the ramblings of the ludicrous, the uproar underlined yet again that Douglas just can't help himself when it comes to upsetting the status quo – but he claims that he doesn't go out of his way to upset the political correct. He just bases his decisions on what makes him laugh or feel angry or upset.

But perhaps even Douglas realised that the public at large needed a change from his dark-edged everyman image – his next choices in film saw Douglas pulling back from his self-confessed "Prince Of Darkness" roles and into something decidedly more presidential.

11

I'm the good guy?

MICHAEL DOUGLAS

I'M THE GOOD GUY?

Michael Douglas had it good, very good. *Disclosure* turned out to be a worldwide hit and more importantly, Douglas became the first Hollywood actor with the power to green-light a movie that he wasn't actually starring in when he formed Constellation Films that had a whopping $500 million to finance 12 films.

He'd also avoided potential career suicide when he eventually turned down the role of shipmate William Shaw alongside Geena Davis in the pirate epic *Cut Throat Island*, a film that would go on to become a box office stinker and the object of much mirth at the dastardly hands of the critics. Instead,

MICHAEL DOUGLAS

I'M THE GOOD GUY?

Douglas kept his trousers pulled up, and took on a much more wholesome role – the character of Andrew Shepherd, the president of the United States. Well, it's wholesome in theory if not in practice but the Bill Clinton/Monica Lewinsky disdainful (and stainful) coupling hadn't materialised on the skirt hem of the world politics scene just yet.

The main role in *The American President* was initially intended for Robert Redford who had been tinkering with the idea of playing the world's most powerful man who secretly heads out of the White House in the pursuit of love but his version *The President Has Eloped!* was more screwball comedy than romantic comedy.

Indeed, when director Rob Reiner came on board and asked Aaron Sorkin to write a new draft, the end result was also a far more political film – and one that Redford lost interest in. Michael Douglas however, probably on the look out for something that didn't revolve around ice picks, leapt at the chance, not concerned about being tarnished with such a political brush. As he told *The San Francisco Chronicle* in 1995: "I guess I don't have such a strong sense of my own persona that I would be too worried that people would be so

I'M THE GOOD GUY?

conscious of myself and my politics."

The American President tells the story of widowed Andrew Shepherd, who has a 12-year-old daughter and a seemingly rock-solid approval rating with his public. Enter Sydney Ellen Wade played by Annette Bening, an environmental lobbyist, and the president finds himself falling in love. Trouble is that the media and opposition politicians – headed by the scene-stealing Richard Dreyfuss as Senator Bob Rumson – try to twist the couple's budding relationship into something all the more nefarious and politically-driven.

During his promotions for the movie, Douglas admitted that it is "every actor's dream is to play the president one time in their career." Taking on such a formidable character also meant submerging himself in research – Douglas read through presidential diaries, spent time with Bill Clinton's staff and on a few occasions, actually hung out with the saxophone player himself. And Clinton himself loved the movie. He even invited Douglas to a real White House reception for President Chirac: "I was in the receiving line, going into dinner. [Then he] came up to me and said, 'Hello, Mr. President.' then added, 'I always wanted to do that. I wondered what it was like.'

I'M THE GOOD GUY?

[Clinton's] a very charming, very bright guy."

While the film itself was warmly received by critics, it didn't set the box office alight and nor did Constellation's remake of *Sabrina* starring Harrison Ford and Julia Ormond which followed a month later and fared far worse – not that Douglas had much to worry about as on the horizon was the box office hit *Face/Off* even if the pricey adaptation of John Grisham's *The Rainmaker* didn't drum up the business expected.

But at the time, Douglas had more important issues to contemplate – his separation from Diandra Douglas. Yet more bad news followed when Kirk Douglas suffered a severe stroke in early 1996 – while the father and son had been lining up to star in their first movie together, *A Song For David*. Sadly, such plans paled into insignificance when Kirk was left unable to walk or talk.

Whatever issues the media have talked up about the difficult nature of the relationship between the two men over the decades, Douglas rallied round his father and in March 1996, encouraged the slowly rehabilitating legend to make a personal appearance at the Oscars in 1996 to accept a Lifetime Achievement Award.

In the meantime, Douglas began producing

I'M THE GOOD GUY?

and acting duties on *The Ghost And The Darkness* in Africa. The story penned by veteran screenwriter William Goldman is based on the true account of two lions that went on a murderous rampage in East Africa, chewing their way through 135 workers constructing a railroad bridge over the Tsavo River during the 1890s.

Val Kilmer, an actor known for frustrating directors, starred as the Irish railway engineer, Colonel John Henry Patterson, who decides that the two lions 'The Ghost' and 'The Darkness' must be shot to stop the killings – and allow the construction of the bridge to continue.

In the film, he is accompanied by Charles Remington who was in fact a composite of the many real-life hunters who joined Patterson on his crusade. While he wasn't intending to play the role, Douglas was happy to take a part that didn't require him to carry an entire film for once – as he told reporters, it felt more like *Wall Street* in a way because the responsibility was on Val Kilmer's shoulders (like Charlie Sheen) to pull the movie off.

Perhaps the biggest problem facing the film though was Disney's *The Lion King* that portrayed nature's most fearsome animals as something decidedly more cuddly. The audience's romantic

I'M THE GOOD GUY?

image of lions didn't sit well with the film's depiction of them as evil spirits. Costing $55 million, *The Ghost And The Darkness* only managed to bring in just under $40 million at the US box office. By this time though, Michael Douglas was busy working on *The Game*, the latest flick from Hollywood's wunderkind director David Fincher who had directed the smash hit *Seven* starring Morgan Freeman and Brad Pitt two years earlier.

Douglas was brought in to play Nicholas Van Orton, a cold and distant über-successful investment banker haunted by the memories of his father's suicide who, for his 48th birthday gift from his younger brother Conrad (played by Sean Penn) is enrolled into a 'game', organised by the mysterious Consumer Recreation Services. Before he has time to breathe, Van Orton finds himself thrown into hell as his assets are stripped from him, his social standing ripped to shreds and his life endangered. Throwing off his normally cautious and calculated nature, Van Orton turns the tables on CRS and in a quite spectacular dénouement, discovers the real purpose of *The Game*.

It was an ideal opportunity for Douglas to build on his Gordon Gekko character from *Wall Street*. The film's production didn't come without

I'M THE GOOD GUY?

the usual problems though – the part of the young brother Conrad played by Sean Penn was originally intended for Jodie Foster but according to Douglas, the problem was that she didn't want to be his sister – but his daughter. Douglas wasn't happy with this, so the role was adapted for Penn.

The casting clash ended up getting ugly when Foster filed a lawsuit for breach of contract against the film's studio, PolyGram. Eventually though, filming got underway. While Fincher and Douglas were wary of each other to begin with – after all, Douglas was old school while Fincher was the new kid on the block – they ended up hitting it off. Douglas explained that they shared some personality traits: "David is a stubborn guy but it comes out of vision. I loved the extent to which he would go to recreate the picture he had in his mind..."

The Game didn't fare well in the States but overseas, it turned in a tidy profit. But just as the central character's life is spinning out of control in *The Game,* so it was for Douglas during the film's shoot. Cameron Douglas, his 17-year-old-son, was arrested for drunk driving and hit-and-run in October 1996. To say it was a wake up call for Douglas as a father is probably an understatement as he shifted his focus from working on big budget

I'M THE GOOD GUY?

movies to his son over the following year.

At this time, Michael and Diandra Douglas were getting divorced – she later told the media that all the time Michael had spent away from home, shooting movies had meant she and Cameron were almost their own separate family unit. As Douglas would jokingly recall in interviews, the divorce probably led him to accept his next role in the remake of Alfred Hitchcock's *Dial M For Murder, A Perfect Murder*.

Playing Steven Taylor, an industrialist with a bank account the size of Nebraska, Douglas discovers that his young trophy wife Emily (played by Gwyneth Paltrow) is playing away with a handsome stud/artist David Shaw. Instead of throwing her out or going for marriage counselling, Taylor decides the best way to play the delicate situation is to blackmail and bribe Shaw into bumping the cheating hussy off.

Yes, it was another one of Douglas's 'Prince of Darkness' roles, which Douglas attacked with glee. "The joy of playing a pure villain is that there is no moral dilemma. Audiences love them because we're all caught up by our civility, our social responsibility, our sense of what's right. It's fun to watch someone who has no sense of that

I'M THE GOOD GUY?

whatsoever just rip it up. There's a little part in all of us that says 'I wish I could do that.'"

By the time *A Perfect Murder* hit the screens, it was announced that Douglas had been appointed United Nations Messenger of Peace in July 1998 by the UN's Secretary General Kofi Annan. Douglas wanted to use his celebrity muscle to highlight two key areas that had concerned him for decades – the proliferation of small arms and his desire for the disarmament of nuclear weapons.

Meanwhile, in his personal life, Douglas was leading the life of a bachelor boy – single again, he moved into his New York apartment, knocking through a wall into the adjourning one to make it bigger. He reflected that sharing the apartment with his 20-year-old son was not exactly where he expected to be at the ripe old age of 53. But that, of course, would all change soon enough.

12

Keeping up with the Zeta-Jones's

MICHAEL DOUGLAS

KEEPING UP WITH THE ZETA-JONES'S

I t's hardly surprising that bachelor 'boy' Douglas had his new-found lifestyle overturned in 1998 – after all, he met Catherine Zeta-Jones. *The Darling Buds Of May* TV star caught Michael Douglas's eye when he'd seen her Hollywood breakout movie *The Mask Of Zorro* two weeks previously: "I was completely wowed by this incredibly beautiful actress I'd never seen before. The last time any actress had done that to me on-screen was Julie Christie."

To make matters even better, *The Mask Of Zorro* was being shown at the French town of Deauville at the Festival Of American Films that

MICHAEL DOUGLAS

KEEPING UP WITH THE ZETA-JONES'S

Douglas was attending to pick up an award for services to the film industry, while also attending the European premiere of *A Perfect Murder*. He discovered through his agent that Catherine Zeta-Jones would also be making an appearance at the festival and more importantly, she wouldn't be turning up with a date.

The two eventually met at a cocktail reception in Deauville, where they hit it off instantly – the established Hollywood legend Douglas famously chatting up the budding starlet with the line that he wanted to be the father of her children. In her favour, well, apart from those smouldering good looks and that now famous hourglass figure, it turned out Jones was also a keen golfer like Douglas, and that they share the same birthday – 25 September.

Although Douglas returned to New York, and Zeta-Jones to Scotland to continue shooting *Entrapment* alongside Sean Connery, the pair remained in touch over the following months, and spent Christmas together in LA, where they were joined by Catherine's parents. While the couple tried to keep the relationship away from the glaring lights and headlines of the Hollywood gossip mill, some six months after their meeting at the cocktail

KEEPING UP WITH THE ZETA-JONES'S

reception in Deauville, they were photographed holidaying at Douglas's villa in Majorca – she topless and he with his arm round her.

The couple's first official appearance together was the European premiere of *Entrapment* in July 1999, where Zeta-Jones sported a diamond ring on her engagement finger that she later claimed she had simply borrowed from a friend but she had already coyly told *Hello!* magazine that Michael had been great to her. "He's given me a lot of support when I've needed a friendly helping hand, and he's a charming guy and a real gentleman."

The media of course spent the next few months speculating wildly as to when the couple would tie the knot. She had, after all, moved into Douglas's New York apartment and they had spent Christmas 1999 together with her family in Mumbles, Wales. The actual announcement of their engagement came in January 2000 when Douglas posted a letter on his official website which declared: "I am very happy to announce that I am engaged to Catherine Zeta-Jones. I proposed to Catherine on New Year's Eve at my house in Aspen. We plan to marry sometime this year, however, no date has been set. Check my Website in the future and you'll be among the first to know."

KEEPING UP WITH THE ZETA-JONES'S

But the media couldn't wait for the official updates on his site and speculated wildly about the date and location of the impending wedding ceremony – the hot favourite was that they would get married in Majorca on their joint birthdays.

But the couple had one more shocker up their sleeves. In late January of the same year, they released an official statement that read: "Catherine Zeta-Jones and Michael Douglas are pleased to announce they are expecting a child. It will be the first child for Ms. Zeta-Jones. Mr. Douglas has a son, Cameron, from a previous marriage."

Baby Dylan Michael Douglas was born on 8 August at 5:52pm in LA and as for any resemblance to his esteemed parents, well, Douglas's publicist Alan Burry would quip about Dylan that "they all look like prunes at this stage."

The couple later released official photos of their new arrival in – a canny move that meant there was less chance of paparazzi door-stepping them. As Douglas revealed later: "[You know] the little baby monitors in your house, right? We can't have them because people outside are tuning into your frequency, trying to listen to your conversations. When you have that kind of insanity going on, we thought, 'All right, we'll take some nice pictures with our kid, and then that will stop. There will be no market for these guys to sell photographs.'"

Three months later saw another press scrum – when Douglas and Zeta-Jones got married in the Terrace Room at the Plaza Hotel in New York on 18 November 2000.

The golden couple tied the knot in front of over 350 people including a veritable who's who of glitterati including Sharon Stone, Kurt Russell, Goldie Hawn, Jack Nicholson, Sir Anthony Hopkins, Russell Crowe, Meg Ryan and Danny DeVito, with best man duties carried out by Cameron Douglas. And best boy's duties by Dylan Douglas.

The day cost around $2 million with $60,000 being blown on the wedding photos alone. The official coupling of Michael Douglas and Catherine Zeta Jones was also celebrated on the other side of the Atlantic in Jones' hometown of Swansea where seafront shops put out flags and bunting.

Perhaps the feelings of married men the world over on the loss of Catherine Zeta-Jones as one of the world's most eligible women, were summed up best by 83-year-old Kirk as he quipped to reporters: "I'd marry her myself, but my wife won't let me."

13

Finally, the family man

MICHAEL DOUGLAS

FINALLY, THE FAMILY MAN

Perhaps it was because of Catherine Zeta-Jones. Or new arrival Dylan. Or perhaps Douglas himself had simply tired of his Prince Of Darkness roles but while the media was chasing its tail over the Douglas-Zeta-Jones relationship, fans noticed that Douglas had mellowed when it came to the roles he was choosing. The Prince Of Darkness was taking some time out.

And this was clearly evident in the comedy drama *Wonder Boys*, directed by Curtis Hanson who was hot from helming the sublime cop drama *LA Confidential*. Based on the book by Michael Chambon, Douglas plays the role of a college professor/frustrated writer Grady Tripp who's under pressure from his editor to finish his second novel. What this meant for Douglas the actor, was that he had to gain 25 pounds and spend most of the film wearing a woman's dirty pink bathrobe – about as far removed from the likes of Gordon Gekko as an actor can get.

As Hanson pointed out Douglas is not an actor known for his vanity: "To play Grady Tripp, I asked Michael to gain 25 pounds, wear the most outrageous clothes and generally look totally dissipated. Most actors of his generation would have walked away."

Douglas commented on his seeming lack of concern about his 'celebrity persona' in an interview: "I've watched too many actors, so concerned with their images or so concerned with trying to make the best portrayal for them, that they ruin what the picture is about."

The film opened to glowing reviews in 2000 and there was even talk of an Oscar nomination for Douglas but, despite the film being re-released later in the year in an attempt to attract the attentions of Academy members, it was not to be.

But it wasn't bad news by any stretch – after all, in the same year, critics applauded Douglas and the rest of the cast of *Traffic*, the film based on the multi-award winning British TV series *Traffik* produced by Channel 4 Films. Michael Douglas had originally turned down the role of Robert Wakefield, a supreme court judge who is appointed America's Drug Czar only to discover that his daughter is in fact hooked on heroin. Indeed, another Hollywood heavyweight, Harrison Ford, accepted the offer and worked with the film's director Steven Soderbergh to flesh out the Wakefield character. Ford though eventually pulled out but Douglas was so enamoured of the new improved Wakefield that he took the role.

Despite a somewhat torturous shoot for director Soderbergh, the film was showered with plaudits on its release in 2000 for its harrowing and insightful look at how drugs affect the lives of a series of people – from Douglas's increasingly disillusioned Wakefield character and Mexican cop Javier Rodriguez (in yet another powerhouse performance from Benicio Del Toro) facing off to his superior's hypocrisy through to two federal agents Ray Castro (played by Luis Guzman) and Montel Gordon (Don Cheadle) whose attempts to bring down a drug smuggler are foiled by his wife – played by one Catherine Zeta-Jones who was

FINALLY, THE FAMILY MAN

very heavily pregnant with Dylan at the time.

While it was the first film the two would star in, fans were disappointed that Douglas and Zeta-Jones didn't actually share any scenes together. But the pundits and box office returns show that the film was both a critical and commercial success. Some wondered if Jones would land herself an Oscar for her portrayal of Helena Ayala in *Traffic*, but that was not the case.

In the meantime, Douglas headed off to cameo in *One Night At McCool's*, a film about three young men who all fall under the spell of femme fatale Liv Tyler on that titular evening. A pompadour-sporting Michael Douglas plays a hitman hired by one of the young bucks to take out Tyler's character. Unfortunately, to say the Douglas-produced film received a beating at the hands of critics and box office alike is something of an understatement.

2001 saw Douglas return to a much more mainstream fare with the thriller *Don't Say A Word* based on the Edgar-Award-winning book by Andrew Klavan. Douglas plays a well-heeled New York shrink, Doctor Nathan Conrad, who must extract information from a young female patient or his kidnapped daughter will be murdered.

MICHAEL DOUGLAS

FINALLY, THE FAMILY MAN

Douglas's character must have felt like a return to *Fatal Attraction*'s Dan Gallagher (but without the infidelity of course) as the everyman who with his back up against the wall, comes out with his pent-up rage flying.

The film was perhaps more significant though because only three weeks before, the world had been rocked by the horrific events on September 11 2001 and *Don't Say A Word* became the first major Hollywood flick to be released in its aftermath – even though it had originally been targeted for a 2002 release. While the final cut saw the shots of the World Trade Center cut from the film apart from one, single long shot, audiences did give the movie a thumbs-up and it made over $54 million at the box office.

The events of September 11 also had a profound effect on Douglas who was in New York with his family at the time – indeed, his 22-year-old-son Cameron witnessed the first tower falling down from his roof. The terrorist attack made Michael Douglas realise just how important his family ties were and resulted in him fast-tracking the film that would unite three generations of the Douglas clan. He claimed that the terrorist attack made his family feel closer and that it made him think about how important each day was. It also made him realise that if he didn't make a film with his father, he wouldn't feel complete.

It Runs In The Family saw both Michael and Kirk plus Douglas's son Cameron share screen time together – and there was also a role for Michael Douglas's mum, Diana. The film follows the trails and tribulations of lawyer Alex Gromberg (played by Michael Douglas) and his difficult relationships with his family – those with his grandparents Mitchell and Evelyn (played by Kirk Douglas and Diana Douglas) and his sons (played by Cameron Douglas and Rory Culkin).

Veteran Aussie director Fred Schepisi was drafted in to helm the picture – himself no stranger to dealing with roomfuls of top drawer actors; 2001 saw the release of *Last Orders* starring Michael Caine, Bob Hoskins and Helen Mirren. Indeed, Schepisi was well aware of the film's potential problem areas: "The first thing I made sure of was that it was a serious project about these fictional characters, and that it wasn't a vanity project," explained Schepisi.

But the film's content could be easily miscon-strued by audiences – after all, at the heart of the story is the son's desire to step out of his father's

FINALLY, THE FAMILY MAN

shadow and garner his dad's respect but as Kirk Douglas said, such a blurring between fact and fiction was bound to happen. And he was keen to point out that there was no overlap between the on-screen and off-screen families, stating that he got along a lot better with Michael than his character in the film did.

While it had taken over 20 years for father and son to finally team up on the big screen, and for all its best intentions, it was unfortunate that the film was neither well received by critics or the cinema-going public – some reviewers labelled it a TV movie of the week. While *It Runs In The Family* may have under-whelmed, it's an essential rental for anyone interested in seeing two Hollywood legends finally sharing scenes together.

Released around the same time was *The In-Laws*, a remake of the 1979 film of the same name. It tells the story of two fathers who meet on the evening of their respective offspring's big day – one is Dr Jerome Peyser played by Albert Brooks, a podiatrist and the other is reckless CIA agent, Steve Tobias, played by Michael Douglas. In the best traditions of screwball comedy, once the two meet up, all hell breaks loose.

"It's been a while since I've done a comedy

film," said Douglas about his role in the film. "*The In-Laws* is broader in its humour than anything I've done before and that's a real treat for me. It's relaxing, not having to keep up that constant tension level you do with a drama."

He would tell reporters how it was difficult performing comedy material with no immediate audience response. "I've done some plays in the past, and when you say 'da da da da,' there's a corresponding 'ha ha ha' from the audience and you move forward. [On a film set], you say 'da da da da' and there's dead silence. It takes some getting used to. In those moments, catching glances of Fleming [the director] at the monitor with his hand over his mouth, suppressing laughter, really helped."

While it was clear that Douglas enjoyed the high jinks of performing the OTT CIA operative character of Steve Tobias, *The In-Laws* only managed to make it to number five in the US's top ten on its release and scraped home with a measly $20 million.

In recent years, Douglas has become better known for his celebrity persona than his on-screen one. With his headline-grabbing marriage to Catherine Zeta-Jones and the subsequent arrival

FINALLY, THE FAMILY MAN

of Dylan, the media regarded the two more as Hollywood royalty than just mere actors. This image was further underlined in 2003 when the world watched Douglas and Zeta-Jones appear in a British court. The lawsuit dated from their wedding in 2000, where the couple had signed a $1.7 million deal with *OK!* magazine that allowed the publication exclusive rights to print pictures of the big day. The only problem was that rival magazine *Hello!* got its own shots on the day and managed to get them out on to the news-stands three days before *OK!*.

The Douglas's filed a lawsuit which culminated in Zeta-Jones taking the stand at the Old Bailey in London to give a 90-minute testimony detailing why she was so upset – she felt that *Hello!*'s shots were "cheap and tacky," that the pictures invaded their privacy, and made her look large. Zeta-Jones felt that such photos were career-damaging for a movie actress whose looks and figure are so important when obtaining roles in Hollywood.

Although cynics suggested that the money the couple made from selling the pictures had to be a factor in bringing the lawsuit against *Hello!* magazine, Zeta-Jones was having none of it, leading her to make her brutally honest but

FINALLY, THE FAMILY MAN

infamous statement: "I get well compensated in my job and my husband has had a long career, financially successful, and it is a lot of money maybe to a lot of people in this room, but it is not that much for us."

In court, Michael Douglas also aired his grievances about *Hello!* magazine's pictures: "We believed that *Hello* was exacting revenge on us because we had decided to provide the rights to publish photographs of our wedding to their competitor. The whole thing was spiteful."

Ultimately, the judge decided that while their "commercial confidence" had been breached, there had been no breach of the Douglas' privacy because no such law exists in the UK. While the couple were demanding over $800,000 for loss of income, stress and damage to their careers, they would ultimately end up being awarded just $24,250 in damages but *Hello!* magazine would later be told to pay a substantial part of the couple's legal costs that came to £4 million.

There was far more important news for Douglas and Zeta-Jones during 2003 though – Zeta-Jones would garner herself a Best Supporting Actress Oscar for her performance in *Chicago* but more importantly, she would give birth to the couple's

FINALLY, THE FAMILY MAN

second child, daughter Carys on 20 April at 4:50am.

With so much of their personal lives making the headlines – and one which shows no sign of abating after the Douglas's legal wranglings over a £1.3 million mansion in Mumbles, Wales and Zeta-Jones changing agent, one could be forgiven for asking when audiences will be seeing the two actually acting on the big screen together.

There was talk of Douglas and Zeta-Jones appearing together in a movie based on the adventures of magician Jean Robert-Houdin in *Smoke And Mirrors*. Then the two were all set to play opposing con artists in the Stephen Frears film *MonkeyFace* but alas, that has now fallen by the way side. Whenever the public do see the two together, it won't be in any steamy scenes *Basic Instinct*-style. After all, Douglas himself has said that it's essential for married actors not to play lovers and that they are looking for projects which don't portray them as a couple.

In the meantime, there are reports that Douglas will take the lead role in *Art Con* (after all, he's already started on the film in a producing role). He's also penned in to produce and act in *The Ride Down Mt Morgan* based on the play by Arthur Miller, and is rumoured to be up for an appearance

FINALLY, THE FAMILY MAN

in *Sin City*, the adaptation of the Frank Miller graphic novel being brought to the big screen by Hollywood maverick Robert Rodriguez.

While ultimately it may seem that Douglas is settling down into the role of a family man these days, there can be no doubt that he's managed to establish himself as a true Hollywood great – something underlined when he was awarded the Cecil B. DeMille Award for outstanding contribution to the entertainment field at the 61st annual Golden Globe awards in 2004.

As for what the future holds for Douglas, well, don't expect the Prince Of Darkness to rest on his laurels – the very thing that defines Douglas the actor and producer is his unerring ability to continually shock, surprise and entertain audiences the world over.

After all, as *One Flew Over The Cuckoo's Nest*, *The China Syndrome*, *Wall Street*, *Falling Down* and the many other films in his glittering portfolio have shown, Michael Douglas is a man who is clearly not afraid to challenge audiences and critics. Or, for that matter, himself.

14

Filmography

MICHAEL DOUGLAS

FILMOGRAPHY

Hail Hero (1969)
Role: Carl Dixon
Producer: Harold D. Cohen
Director: David Miller
Screenwriter: David Manber
Key cast: Arthur Kennedy, Teresa Wright,
John Larch, Charles Drake

Adam At 6AM (1970)
Role: Adam Gaines
Producers: Rick Rosenberg and
Robert W Christiansen
Director: Robert Scheerer
Screenwriters: Elinor Karpf and Steven Karpf
Key cast: Lee Purcell, Joe Don Baker,
Louise Latham, Meg Foster

Summertree (1971)
Role: Jerry
Producer: Kirk Douglas
Director: Anthony Newley
Screenwriters: Ron Cowen, Edward Hume and
Stephen Yafa
Key cast: Jack Warden, Brenda Vaccaro,
Barbara Bel Geddes

MICHAEL DOUGLAS

FILMOGRAPHY

Napoleon And Samantha (1972)
Role: Danny
Producer: Winston Hibler
Director: Bernard McEveety
Screenwriter: Stewart Raffill
Key cast: Johnny Whitaker, Jodie Foster,
Will Geer

Coma (1978)
Role: Dr Mark Bellows
Producer: Martin Erlichman
Director: Michael Crichton
Screenwriter: Michael Crichton
Key cast: Geneieve Bujold, Elizabeth Ashley,
Rip Torn

The China Syndrome (1979)
Role: Richard Adams
Producer: Michael Douglas
Director: James Bridges
Screenwriters: Mike Gray, T S Cook and
James Bridges
Key cast: Jane Fonda, Jack Lemmon,
Scott Brady, James Hampton

MICHAEL DOUGLAS

FILMOGRAPHY

Running (1979)
Role: Michael Andropolis
Producers: Ronald I. Cohen and Robert M. Cooper
Director: Steve Hilliard Stern
Screenwriter: Steve Hilliard Stern
Key cast: Susan Anspach, Lawrence Dane,
Philips Akin

It's My Turn (1980)
Role: Ben Lewin
Producer: Martin Elfand
Director: Claudia Weill
Screenwriter: Eleanor Bergstein
Key cast: Jill Clayburgh, Charles Grodin,
Beverly Garland,

The Star Chamber (1983)
Role: Superior Court Judge Steven R. Hardin
Producer: Frank Yablans
Director: Peter Hyams
Screenwriter: Roderick Taylor
Key cast: Hal Holbrook, Yaphet Kotto,
Sharon Gless

MICHAEL DOUGLAS

FILMOGRAPHY

Romancing The Stone (1984)
Role: Jack T. Colton
Producer: Michael Douglas
Director: Robert Zemeckis
Screenwriter: Diane Thomas
Key cast: Kathleen Turner, Danny DeVito,
Zack Norman, Alfonso Arau

A Chorus Line (1985)
Role: Zach
Producers: Cy Feuer and Ernest H. Martin
Director: Richard Attenborough
Screenwriter: Arnold Schulman
Key cast: Alyson Reed, Terrance Mann,
Janet Jones

The Jewel Of The Nile (1985)
Role: Jack T. Colton
Producer: Michael Douglas
Director: Lewis Teague
Screenwriters: Mark Rosenthal and
Lawrence Konner
Key cast: Kathleen Turner, Danny DeVito,
Spiros Focas, Avner Eisenberg

MICHAEL DOUGLAS

FILMOGRAPHY

Fatal Attraction (1987)
Role: Dan Gallagher
Producers: Sherry Lansing and Stanley Jaffe
Director: Adrian Lyne
Screenwriters: James Dearden and Nicholas Meyer
Key cast: Glenn Close, Anne Archer,
Ellen Hamilton Latzen

Wall Street (1987)
Role: Gordon Gekko
Producer: Edward R. Pressman
Director: Oliver Stone
Screenwriters: Stanley Weiser and Oliver Stone
Key cast: Charlie Sheen, Daryl Hannah,
Martin Sheen, Terence Stamp

Black Rain (1989)
Role: Nick
Producers: Sherry Lansing and Stanley Jaffe
Director: Ridley Scott
Screenwriters: Craig Bolotin and Warren Lewis
Key cast: Andy Garcia, Ken Takakura,
Yusaka Matsuda

MICHAEL DOUGLAS

FILMOGRAPHY

The War Of The Roses (1989)
Role: Oliver Rose
Producers: James L. Brooks and Arnon Milchan
Director: Danny DeVito
Screenwriter: Michael Leeson
Key cast: Kathleen Turner, Danny DeVito,
Sean Astin

Shining Through (1991)
Role: Ed Leland
Producers: Carol Baum and Howard Rosenman
Director: David Seltzer
Screenwriter: David Seltzer
Key cast: Melanie Griffith, Liam Neeson,
Joely Richardson, John Gielgud

Basic Instinct (1991)
Role: Dect. Nick Curran
Producer: Alan Marshall
Director: Paul Verhoeven
Screenwriter: Joe Eszterhas
Key cast: Sharon Stone, George Dzundza,
Jeanne Tripplehorn

MICHAEL DOUGLAS

FILMOGRAPHY

Falling Down (1993)
Role: D-Fens
Producers: Timothy Harris, Arnold Kopelson and
Herschel Weingrod
Director: Joel Shumacher
Screenwriter: Ebbe Roe Smith
Key cast: Robert Duvall, Barbara Hershey,
Tuesday Weld

Disclosure (1994)
Role: Tom Sanders
Producer: Barry Levinson
Director: Barry Levinson
Screenwriter: Paul Attanasio
Key cast: Demi Moore, Donald Sutherland,
Caroline Goodall

The American President (1995)
Role: President Andrew Shepherd
Producer: Rob Reiner
Director: Rob Reiner
Screenwriter: Aaron Sorkin
Key cast: Annette Bening, Martin Sheen,
Michael J. Fox

MICHAEL DOUGLAS

FILMOGRAPHY

The Ghost And The Darkness
Role: Charles Remington
Producers: A. Kitman Ho, Gale Anne Hurd and
Paul B. Radin
Director: Stephen Hopkins
Screenwriter: William Goldman
Key cast: Val Kilmer, Tom Wilkinson,
Emily Mortimer

The Game (1997)
Role: Nicholas Van Orton
Producers: Cean Chaffin and Steve Golin
Director: David Fincher
Screenwriters: John D. Brancato and
Michael Ferris
Key cast: Sean Penn, Deborah Kara Unger,
James Rebhorn

A Perfect Murder (1998)
Role: Steven Taylor
Producers: Anne Kopelson, Arnold Kopelson, Peter
MacGregor-Scott and Christopher Mankiewicz
Director: Andrew Davis
Screenwriter: Patrick Smith Kelly
Key cast: Gwyneth Paltrow, Viggo Mortensen,
David Suchet

MICHAEL DOUGLAS

FILMOGRAPHY

Wonder Boys (2000)
Role: Grady Tripp
Producers: Curtis Hanson and Scott Rudin
Director: Curtis Hanson
Screenwriter: Steve Kloves
Key cast: Robert Downey Jnr., Tobey Maguire,
Katie Holmes

Traffic (2000)
Role: Robert Hudson Wakefield
Producers: Laura Bickford, Marshall Herskowitz
and Edward Zwick
Director: Steven Soderbergh
Screenwriter: Stephen Gaghan
Key cast: Catherine Zeta-Jones, Benicio Del Toro,
Salma Hayek

One Night At McCool's (2001)
Role: Mr Burmeister
Producers: Michael Douglas and
Allison Lyon Segan
Director: Harald Zwart
Screenwriter: Stan Seidel
Key cast: Liv Tyler, Matt Dillon, John Goodman

FILMOGRAPHY

Don't Say A Word (2001)
Role: Dr. Nathan R. Conrad
Producers: Anne Kopelson, Arnold Kopelson and
Arnon Milchan
Director: Gary Fleder
Screenwriter: Anthony Peckham and
Patrick Smith Kelly
Key cast: Brittany Murphy, Famke Janssen,
Sean Bean

It Runs In The Family (2003)
Role: Alex Gromberg
Producer: Michael Douglas
Director: Fred Schepisi
Screenwriter: Jesse Wigutow
Key cast: Kirk Douglas, Cameron Douglas,
Rory Culkin, Diana Douglas

The In-Laws (2003)
Role: Steve Tobias
Producers: Bill Gerber, Elie Samaha, Joel Simon
and Bill Todman Jnr.
Director: Andrew Fleming
Screenwriters: Nat Mauldin and Ed Solomon
Key cast: Albert Brooks, Candice Bergen, Ryan
Reynolds

MICHAEL DOUGLAS

FILMOGRAPHY

Also as Producer, Co-Producer or Executive Producer:

One Flew Over The Cuckoo's Nest (1975)
Starman (1984)
Flatliners (1990)
Stone Cold (1991)
Double Impact (1991)
Eyes Of An Angel (1991)
Radio Flyer (1992)
Made In America (1993)
The Rainmaker (1997)
Face/Off (1997)
Godspeed, Lawrence Mann (2004)
Ride Down To Mt. Morgan (2005)
Art Con (2005)

BIOGRAPHIES

OTHER BOOKS IN THE SERIES

Also available in the series:

OTHER BOOKS IN THE SERIES

JENNIFER ANISTON

She's been a Friend to countless millions worldwide, and overcame numerous hurdles to rise to the very top of her field. From a shy girl with a dream of being a famous actress, through being reduced to painting scenery for high school plays, appearing in a series of flop TV shows and one rather bad movie, Jennifer Aniston has persevered, finally finding success at the very top of the TV tree.

Bringing the same determination that got her a part on the world's best-loved TV series to her attempts at a film career, she's also worked her way from rom-com cutie up to serious, respected actress and box office draw, intelligently combining indie, cult and comedy movies into a blossoming career which looks set to shoot her to the heights of Hollywood's A-list. She's also found love with one of the world's most desirable men. Is Jennifer Aniston the ultimate Hollywood Renaissance woman? It would seem she's got more than a shot at such a title, as indeed, she seems to have it all, even if things weren't always that way. Learn all about Aniston's rise to fame in this compelling biography.

OTHER BOOKS IN THE SERIES

DAVID BECKHAM

This book covers the amazing life of the boy from East London who has not only become a world class footballer and the captain of England, but also an idol to millions, and probably the most famous man in Britain.

His biography tracks his journey, from the playing fields of Chingford to the Bernabau. It examines how he joined his beloved Manchester United and became part of a golden generation of talent that led to United winning trophies galore.

Beckham's parallel personal life is also examined, as he moved from tongue-tied football-obsessed kid to suitor of a Spice Girl, to one half of Posh & Becks, the most famous celebrity couple in Britain – perhaps the world. His non-footballing activities, his personal indulgences and changing styles have invited criticism, and even abuse, but his football talent has confounded the critics, again and again.

The biography looks at his rise to fame and his relationship with Posh, as well as his decision to leave Manchester for Madrid. Has it affected his relationship with Posh? What will the latest controversy over his sex life mean for celebrity's royal couple? And will he come back to play in England again?

OTHER BOOKS IN THE SERIES

GEORGE CLOONEY

The tale of George Clooney's astonishing career is an epic every bit as riveting as one of his blockbuster movies. It's a story of tenacity and determination, of fame and infamy, a story of succeeding on your own terms regardless of the risks. It's also a story of emergency rooms, batsuits, tidal waves and killer tomatoes, but let's not get ahead of ourselves.

Born into a family that, by Sixties' Kentucky standards, was dripping with show business glamour, George grew up seeing the hard work and heartache that accompanied a life in the media spotlight.

By the time stardom came knocking for George Clooney, it found a level-headed and mature actor ready and willing to embrace the limelight, while still indulging a lifelong love of partying and practical jokes. A staunchly loyal friend and son, a bachelor with a taste for the high life, a vocal activist for the things he believes and a born and bred gentleman; through failed sitcoms and blockbuster disasters, through artistic credibility and box office success, George Clooney has remained all of these things...and much, much more. Prepare to meet Hollywood's most fascinating megastar in this riveting biography.

OTHER BOOKS IN THE SERIES

BILLY CONNOLLY

In a 2003 London Comedy Poll to find Britain's favourite comedian, Billy Connolly came out on top. It's more than just Billy Connolly's all-round comic genius that puts him head and shoulders above the rest. Connolly has also proved himself to be an accomplished actor with dozens of small and big screen roles to his name. In 2003, he could be seen in *The Last Samurai* with Tom Cruise.

Connolly has also cut the mustard in the USA, 'breaking' that market in a way that chart-topping pop groups since The Beatles and the Stones have invariably failed to do, let alone mere stand-up comedians. Of course, like The Beatles and the Stones, Billy Connolly has been to the top of the pop charts too with D.I.V.O.R.C.E. in 1975.

On the way he's experienced heartache of his own with a difficult childhood and a divorce of his own, found the time and energy to bring up five children, been hounded by the press on more than one occasion, and faced up to some considerable inner demons. But Billy Connolly is a survivor. Now in his 60s, he's been in show business for all of 40 years, and 2004 finds him still touring. This exciting biography tells the story an extraordinary entertainer.

OTHER BOOKS IN THE SERIES

ROBERT DE NIRO

Robert De Niro is cinema's greatest chameleon. Snarling one minute, smirking the next, he's straddled Hollywood for a quarter of a century, making his name as a serious character actor, in roles ranging from psychotic taxi drivers to hardened mobsters. The scowls and pent-up violence may have won De Niro early acclaim but, ingeniously, he's now playing them for laughs, poking fun at the tough guy image he so carefully cultivated. Ever the perfectionist, De Niro holds nothing back on screen, but in real life he is a very private man – he thinks of himself as just another guy doing a job. Some job, some guy. There's more to the man than just movies. De Niro helped New York pick itself up after the September 11 terrorist attacks on the Twin Towers by launching the TriBeCa Film Festival and inviting everyone downtown. He runs several top-class restaurants and has dated some of the most beautiful women in the world, least of all supermodel Naomi Campbell. Now in his 60s, showered with awards and a living legend, De Niro's still got his foot on the pedal. There are six, yes six, films coming your way in 2004. In this latest biography, you'll discover all about his latest roles and the life of this extraordinary man.

OTHER BOOKS IN THE SERIES

HUGH GRANT

He's the Oxford fellow who stumbled into acting, the middle-class son of a carpet salesman who became famous for bumbling around stately homes and posh weddings. The megastar actor who claims he doesn't like acting, but has appeared in over 40 movies and TV shows.

On screen he's romanced a glittering array of Hollywood's hottest actresses, and tackled medical conspiracies and the mafia. Off screen he's hogged the headlines with his high profile girlfriend as well as finding lifelong notoriety after a little Divine intervention in Los Angeles.

Hugh Grant is Britain's biggest movie star, an actor whose talent for comedy has often been misjudged by those who assume he simply plays himself.

From bit parts in Nottingham theatre, through comedy revues at the Edinburgh Fringe, and on to the top of the box office charts, Hugh has remained constant – charming, witty and ever so slightly sarcastic, obsessed with perfection and performance while winking to his audience as if to say: "This is all awfully silly, isn't it?" Don't miss this riveting biography.

OTHER BOOKS IN THE SERIES

MICHAEL JACKSON

Friday 29 August 1958 was not a special day in Gary, Indiana, and indeed Gary, was far from being a special place. But it was on this day and in this location that the world's greatest entertainer was to be born, Michael Joseph Jackson.

The impact that this boy was destined to have on the world of entertainment could never have been estimated. Here we celebrate Michael Jackson's extraordinary talents, and plot the defining events over his 40-year career. This biography explores the man behind the myth, and gives an understanding of what drives this special entertainer.

In 1993, there was an event that was to rock Jackson's world. His friendship with a 12-year-old boy and the subsequent allegations resulted in a lawsuit, a fall in record sales and a long road to recovery. Two marriages, three children and 10 years later there is a feeling of déjà vu as Jackson again deals with more controversy. Without doubt, 2004 proves to be the most important year in the singer's life. Whatever that future holds for Jackson, his past is secured, there has never been and there will never again be anything quite like Michael Jackson.

OTHER BOOKS IN THE SERIES

NICOLE KIDMAN

On 23 March 2003 Nicole Kidman won the Oscar for Best Actress for her role as Virginia Woolf in *The Hours.* That was the night that marked Nicole Kidman's acceptance into the upper echelons of Hollywood royalty. She had certainly come a long way from the 'girlfriend' roles she played when she first arrived in Hollywood – in films such as *Billy Bathgate* and *Batman Forever* – although even then she managed to inject her 'pretty girl' roles with an edge that made her acting stand out. And she was never merely content to be Mrs Cruise, movie star's wife. Although she stood dutifully behind her then husband in 1993 when he was given his star on the Hollywood Walk of Fame, Nicole got a star of her own 10 years later, in 2003.

Not only does Nicole Kidman have stunning good looks and great pulling power at the box office, she also has artistic credibility. But Nicole has earned the respect of her colleagues, working hard and turning in moving performances from a very early age. Although she dropped out of school at 16, no one doubts the intelligence and passion that are behind the fiery redhead's acting career, which includes television and stage work, as well as films. Find out how Kidman became one of Hollywood's most respected actresses in this compelling biography.

OTHER BOOKS IN THE SERIES

JENNIFER LOPEZ

There was no suggestion that the Jennifer Lopez of the early Nineties would become the accomplished actress, singer and icon that she is today. Back then she was a dancer on the popular comedy show *In Living Color* – one of the Fly Girls, the accompaniment, not the main event. In the early days she truly was Jenny from the block; the Bronx native of Puerto Rican descent – another hopeful from the east coast pursuing her dreams in the west.

Today, with two marriages under her belt, three multi-platinum selling albums behind her and an Oscar-winning hunk as one of her ex-boyfriends, she is one of the most talked about celebrities of the day. Jennifer Lopez is one of the most celebrated Hispanic actresses of all time.

Her beauty, body and famous behind, are lusted after by men and envied by women throughout the world. She has proven that she can sing, dance and act. Yet her critics dismiss her as a diva without talent. And the criticisms are not just about her work, some of them are personal. But what is the reality? Who is Jennifer Lopez, where did she come from and how did get to where she is now? This biography aims to separate fact from fiction to reveal the real Jennifer Lopez.

OTHER BOOKS IN THE SERIES

MADONNA

Everyone thought they had Madonna figured out in early 2003. The former Material Girl had become Maternal Girl, giving up on causing controversy to look after her two children and set up home in England with husband Guy Ritchie. The former wild child had settled down and become respectable. The new Madonna would not do anything to shock the establishment anymore, she'd never do something like snogging both Britney Spears and Christina Aguilera at the MTV Video Music Awards... or would she?

Of course she would. Madonna has been constantly reinventing herself since she was a child, and her ability to shock even those who think they know better is both a tribute to her business skills and the reason behind her staying power. Only Madonna could create gossip with two of the current crop of pop princesses in August and then launch a children's book in September. In fact, only Madonna would even try.

In her 20-year career she has not just been a successful pop singer, she is also a movie star, a business woman, a stage actress, an author and a mother. Find out all about this extraordinary modern-day icon in this new compelling biography.

OTHER BOOKS IN THE SERIES

BRAD PITT

From the launch pad that was his scene stealing turn in *Thelma And Louise* as the sexual-enlightening bad boy. To his character-driven performances in dramas such as *Legends of the Fall* through to his Oscar-nominated work in *Twelve Monkeys* and the dark and razor-edged Tyler Durden in *Fight Club*, Pitt has never rested on his laurels. Or his good looks.

And the fact that his love life has garnered headlines all over the world hasn't hindered Brad Pitt's profile away from the screen either – linked by the press to many women, his relationships with the likes of Juliette Lewis and Gwyneth Paltrow. Then of course, in 2000, we had the Hollywood fairytale ending when he tied the silk knot with Jennifer Aniston.

Pitt's impressive track record as a superstar, sex symbol *and* credible actor looks set to continue as he has three films lined up for release over the next year – as Achilles in the Wolfgang Peterson-helmed *Troy*; Rusty Ryan in the sequel *Ocean's Twelve* and the titular Mr Smith in the thriller *Mr & Mrs Smith* alongside Angelina Jolie. Pitt's ever-growing success shows no signs of abating. Discover all about Pitt's meteoric rise from rags to riches in this riveting biography.

OTHER BOOKS IN THE SERIES

SHANE RICHIE

Few would begrudge the current success of 40-year-old Shane Richie. To get where he is today, Shane has had a rather bumpy roller coaster ride that has seen the hard working son of poor Irish immigrants endure more than his fair share of highs and lows – financially, professionally and personally.

In the space of four decades he has amused audiences at school plays, realised his childhood dream of becoming a Pontins holiday camp entertainer, experienced homelessness, beat his battle with drink, became a millionaire then lost the lot. He's worked hard and played hard.

When the producers of *EastEnders* auditioned Shane for a role in the top TV soap, they decided not to give him the part, but to create a new character especially for him. That character was Alfie Moon, manager of the Queen Vic pub, and very quickly Shane's TV alter ego has become one of the most popular soap characters in Britain. This biography is the story of a boy who had big dreams and never gave up on turning those dreams into reality

OTHER BOOKS IN THE SERIES

JONNY WILKINSON

"There's 35 seconds to go, this is the one. It's coming back for Jonny Wilkinson. He drops for World Cup glory. It's over! He's done it! Jonny Wilkinson is England's Hero yet again..."

That memorable winning drop kick united the nation, and lead to the start of unprecedented victory celebrations throughout the land. In the split seconds it took for the ball to leave his boot and slip through the posts, Wilkinson's life was to change forever. It wasn't until three days later, when the squad flew back to Heathrow and were met with a rapturous reception, that the enormity of their win, began to sink in.

Like most overnight success stories, Wilkinson's journey has been a long and dedicated one. He spent 16 years 'in rehearsal' before achieving his finest performance, in front of a global audience of 22 million, on that rainy evening in Telstra Stadium, Sydney.

But how did this modest self-effacing 24-year-old become England's new number one son? This biography follows Jonny's journey to international stardom. Find out how he caught the rugby bug, what and who his earliest influences were and what the future holds for our latest English sporting hero.

OTHER BOOKS IN THE SERIES

ROBBIE WILLIAMS

Professionally, things can't get much better for Robbie Williams. In 2002 he signed the largest record deal in UK history when he re-signed with EMI. The following year he performed to over 1.5 million fans on his European tour, breaking all attendance records at Knebworth with three consecutive sell-out gigs.

Since going solo Robbie Williams has achieved five number one hit singles, five number one hit albums; 10 Brits and three Ivor Novello awards. When he left the highly successful boy band Take That in 1995 his future seemed far from rosy. He got off to a shaky start. His nemesis, Gary Barlow, had already recorded two number one singles and the press had virtually written Williams off. But then in December 1997, he released his Christmas single, *Angels.*

Angels re-launched his career – it remained in the Top 10 for 11 weeks. Since then Robbie has gone from strength to strength, both as a singer and a natural showman. His live videos are a testament to his performing talent and his promotional videos are works of art.

This biography tells of Williams' journey to the top – stopping off on the way to take a look at his songs, his videos, his shows, his relationships, his rows, his record deals and his demons.